# DON'T GET *Engaged*

## (UNTIL YOU READ THIS BOOK)

### FOUR STEPS OVER FOUR WEEKENDS
*to help you make the
most important decision
in your life!*

by
*Laura Nielson Denke MA, LMHC, LMFT*

Edited by
Conrad W. Denke

Laura Nielson Denke

## Dedicated to:
Conrad, for his encouraging words and unwavering faith in me.

## And Special Thanks to:
Lyndsey Aponik

Xander Denke

Megan Larson

Holly Metcalf

Jimmy Olson

Valerie Payne

Charlotte R. Smith

Printed in the United States of America

1ˢᵗ printing 2019

Library of Congress Control Number: 2019947629

ISBN: 978-0-9673865-8-4

Design and Layout by www.Delaney-Designs.com
Images by canstockphotos/shutterstock
Published by American Press Services

## Publisher's Note

***Don't Get Engaged (until you read this book)*** is designed to help individuals and couples focus on what's important and required for a successful relationship. The book is applicable to those who are currently in a relationship and contemplating getting engaged, those who have been divorced and are hesitant to make another commitment, singles needing a guide for finding an ideal mate, individuals who have been in a long-term unmarried relationship who want to analyze their situation in more detail, and individuals who, early in a relationship, want some direction and guidance. Although the questionnaires and counsel outlined in this book are not an exact science, together they create an invaluable tool to help individuals make good decisions about marriage.

Although the concepts presented in *Don't Get Engaged (until you read this book)* can and will be of great help to most pre-engaged couples, some may require professional counseling and/ or other kinds of help. Individuals who suffer from drug or alcohol addiction should seek safety and counsel through church, city, county, and state agencies before contemplating a serious relationship.

This book is not intended to assist in the treatment of psychiatric disorders. Those who may be suffering from depression or other mood disorders, anxiety disorders, or other psychiatric disorders should seek professional consultation from licensed professionals such as psychiatrists, physicians, and psychologists. Unless these are addressed, any relationship will be problematic.

*Don't Get Engaged (until you read this book)* is a treasure of activities that will help you make wise decisions. Good luck and enjoy the process.

## About the Author

**LAURA NIELSON DENKE** earned a B.A. from Brigham Young University and a Master's degree in Mental Health Counseling from Argosy University Seattle. She is a licensed Marriage and Family Therapist in California and a Licensed Mental Health Counselor in Washington State. She also holds a national certification in Mental Health Counseling. Laura is the author of *Ten Secrets for a Successful Celestial Marriage, Before Your Wedding* and now *Don't Get Engaged (until you read this book)*. Mrs. Denke has twenty-five years of experience counseling married couples. She is especially well known for her thorough pre-marital and pre-engagement counseling.

In Laura's earlier career, prior to becoming a therapist, she choreographed summer stock musical theatre in Lake Placid, New York, taught choreography for the musical stage at Seattle Pacific University and Seattle University, directed and choreographed dozens of ballets for her Seattle Children's Ballet Company including *The Nutcracker Suite, Cinderella, Giselle, Coppelia, Peter and the Wolf* and many others. Her students have performed in Spain and Portugal, and Laura was the first ballet instructor to bring a group of American students to the old Soviet Union to study the Vaganova method of ballet.

Laura and her husband founded Victory Studios with offices in Seattle and Los Angeles. Laura continues to serve as its Executive Vice-President. She wrote and directed the children's special for television entitled *Adventures on Sinclair Island,* broadcast in many countries around the world. Laura was the innovator and host for the television series *Teens Talk*. The series of 39 episodes aired in 160 cities around the US for four years. She wrote and directed other productions for various corporate and charitable organizations and has won several awards for her outstanding directing ability including a Telly Award and Cine Golden Eagle Award.

Laura has a YouTube series called *Relationship Talk With Laura* and is currently executive producer with her husband on the weekly television program, *"Band in Seattle."*

Laura divides her time between her private counseling offices in Seattle and Los Angeles.

# PREFACE

### Why should I read this book before I get engaged?

Getting engaged is a big step. It says that the two of you have decided to spend your lives together as a married couple. It's the most important decision you make in life. But fear of such a big commitment often creates inordinate stress and doubt. Is he or she really the right one? All around you are failed marriages and you wonder how two people who seemed to love each other so much could end up in bitter divorce. My many years of counseling couples in conflict have proven that most problems in marriage could have been prevented. Unfortunately, many think that if they just live together, they'll discover everything they need to know. My experience says that just isn't the case. Understanding someone else is complex because people are complex. Assuming that you know someone can get you in a lot of trouble. We all need to know how to truly get to know someone else before we make a commitment. This book will show you how.

For the past ten years I have seen an increase in couples that live together for a long time but don't marry, and also those that get engaged but can't seem to complete their vows. Some end up in my office unhappy, disillusioned, and desperate. They ask: "Why won't he or she commit? I'm ready. Why isn't he or she?"

*Jessica was eager to get married. She had been engaged for five years and her fiancé repeatedly delayed the marriage. She complained, "Laura, I'm 35 years old, my biological clock is ticking, I want to have children before it's too late."*

*"Why do you think he delays the wedding?" I queried.*

*"Well," she replied sheepishly, "I guess I'm not good enough for him."*

*"What does that mean?" I enquired.*

*"He calls me rude names because I talk to some friends who are male. You know, like at the gym or at my cooking club. He tells me how stupid I am, that I can't do anything right, and that he should dump me, and will if I don't shape up. I really want to get married. I love him."*

*As we talked further, I found out that her fiancé verbally abused her daily. She told me that she grew up in a verbally abusive, alcoholic home and never had the opportunity to see what a normal loving relationship looked like. I helped her to understand that this relationship was harmful to her mental health. Over the course of therapy, she developed higher self-esteem and broke off the engagement and moved out. A year later she met a wonderful man who passed my time-tested pre-engagement course with flying colors! I'm happy to report they are now happily married.*

By doing your homework now, you can avoid great heartache in the future. It is far easier to break off a relationship than to call off an engagement and/or wedding.

Be wise. Do your homework now! And remember these truths: 1. You can fall in love with many different people, even those with which you have nothing in common, whose values are opposite to yours, and whose interests are completely different. However, that doesn't mean you should marry them. 2. Love alone is not a good reason to get married. 3. Love does not conquer all or solve all problems. 4. Marriage requires work. 5. The more you know about each other the better chance for a successful relationship. Marriage is a partnership created to build an everlasting life of friendship, support, family, trust, and meaningful shared activities and experiences.

As you go through this book you will discover whether you have the right ingredients to create a successful engagement and marriage.

# TABLE OF CONTENTS

Four Steps in 4 weekends to know if it's right.

# GENERAL INSTRUCTIONS

This is a workbook with an emphasis on "work." If you follow the instructions carefully, you will be taken through a process that will reveal all the information you need to make an enlightened decision about your relationship, and you'll have fun doing it. I would warn you, however, that the process can be corrupted if you don't avoid three deadly issues: "wanting too much to be liked," "second guessing," and "manipulation." If even one of these intrudes, you will receive inaccurate and misleading results.

The best way for you and your partner to accomplish this work is for you to each have a copy of the book. If that is not possible, just copy the questionnaires for your partner. Filling out the questionnaires separately helps to ensure honest and candid answers. This will help you avoid the three deadly issues. If done together, your partner's answers may be what he/she guesses you would say and not what he/she really thinks: "wanting too much to be liked." If you are together, it is too easy to be swayed or influenced by a verbal opinion from your partner or trying to think what the answer "should" be: "second guessing." In a romantic atmosphere together, you or your partner might say, "Oh yeah, I think that too," even though the exact opposite is true: "manipulation." It's important you avoid these issues and answer the questions honestly and <u>alone</u>.

Here's what happens when one person is dishonest at the beginning of a relationship: *Claire from Los Angeles was looking forward to meeting Jackson, her perfect match according to an Internet dating site. Both Jackson and Claire had independently filled out a thorough questionnaire revealing each one's religious preference, regular sports activities, political persuasion, habits, and much more. Jackson lined up with all her likes and dislikes and Claire became confident that this would be a match made in heaven.*

*After a month of dating, Claire was disappointed. On the first date Jackson lit up a cigarette after dinner. She said, "Your profile said that you didn't smoke." "That's right," Jackson admitted. "I said that I was non-smoking because I'm going to quit." Then it turned out that Jackson wasn't really a Christian as it said on the questionnaire. He believed that all religions were the same. Claire did not. He said he liked to play tennis, but when they had a tennis date, he grumbled the whole time. Fortunately, Claire discovered the truth during active dating, well before she made any commitment, and terminated the relationship. Others are often not that lucky and find out too late.*

During the process of completing the steps in the book, it is important to talk about what is real at the present time. You may also talk about what you would like to become, but don't deviate from who you really are, and what your life is like now!

There are four steps in the book. Each step contains an introduction, instructions including preparation, planning, one or more activities and other assignments, questionnaires and "concepts to consider." The process for each step is simple. **First:** Read the introduction and everything in the step. Fill out the questionnaires <u>separately</u> from your partner. **Second:** Follow the plan including preparation, planning and doing the activities and assignments. **Third:** Review your answers to the questionnaires <u>together</u> as instructed. Summarize where you agree and where you don't and analyze where compromises can or cannot happen. **Fourth:** At the end of each step, review what you have done, <u>alone</u>, and decide if you are ready to take the next step.

And perhaps the most important part, make this fun. It's worth it.

Laura Nielson Denke

# WHO ARE YOU?

# STEP #1 WHO ARE YOU?

## INTRODUCTION

It's critical to clarify who <u>you</u> are before you can understand and know what you need in a lifetime partner. You will have fun finding out or confirming in your mind who you are by filling out the questionnaires in this step. It will make it easier to analyze what you need in an ideal mate. Opposites often attract each other. Sparks fly and emotions run high. Many couples marry because they are just attracted to each other physically. If that's all there is holding them together, within that first year or so of marriage, they often regret the decision as the flame burns out leaving the couple with nothing in common. A famous example of opposites is actress Marilyn Monroe and playwright Arthur Miller. Although they both had a love for theater and movies, their personality types were opposites and the marriage eventually dissolved. This will never happen to you if you honestly complete the FOUR STEPS. Enjoy analyzing yourself, and what you want and need in a mate.

# STEP #1
## INSTRUCTIONS

1. **Preparation:**
   a. Read the entire step.
   b. Individually complete The Personality Profile and questionnaires 1 through 8.

2. **Plan:**
   a. Each of you select a favorite activity for which you are truly passionate. It could be playing football, playing board games, hiking in the woods, playing tennis, ballroom dancing, playing video games, swimming, bicycling, putting together puzzles, cross country skiing, working out at the gym or any other activity that you would want to share with your partner.
   b. For lunch and the afternoon, plan an activity at a local beach or park, lodge or fireplace at home, depending on the weather and time of year. If you go to a beach, bring beach towels to sit on. You could bring a picnic lunch and spread a blanket outdoors or inside in front of a fireplace. Bring your book with completed questionnaires and something to write with.

3. **Activity 1: Participate in the planned activities.**
   a. In the morning of a Saturday or a day you both have available, go on the two prearranged favorite activities together, ones that you both plan on continuing for most of your life. Start early enough to get both activities completed in a morning.

4. **Activity 2: Have lunch and a long discussion.**
   a. Go to the planned location for lunch and take along your books with answered questionnaires. First discuss your dominant personality types and any potential conflicts. Then share and discuss the other questionnaires.
   b. Note what you have in common and any conflicts or disagreements.
   c. Have fun.

5. **AFTER:**
   a. That evening, <u>alone</u>, make notes in your journal about the day, where things went well, where you discovered differences, and if you saw any potential conflicts. (Journal pages are included at the back of the book.)

# PERSONALITY PROFILE

*"To create a great relationship, you must respect, accept, and embrace the differences in each other's personality."*

**PERSONALITY PROFILE**

**Fill out each statement below by circling the one answer that you think best matches the way you think. Many of the answers will apply to you some of the time. Circle the one answer that describes you most of the time.**

1. I like to:
    a. Direct others.
    b. Cooperate with others.
    c. Motivate others.
    d. Follow others as long as the instructions are clear.

2. I prefer to:
    a. Compete in an event.
    b. Cheer for others.
    c. Create the event.
    d. Keep track of the details of the event.

3. I prefer to:
    a. Assign the chores for others to do.
    b. Gladly do the chores no one else will do just to keep peace.
    c. Do chores on my own time schedule.
    d. Read instructions on how to do the chores properly and then do them.

4. My clothes closet:
    a. Is organized, but I'm too busy to think about it much.
    b. Is organized so I know what I'm wearing each day.
    c. Is messy and unorganized, but I always look good.
    d. Is organized according to item, color and texture.

5. I would rather help a friend by:
    a. Solving his/her problem.
    b. Listening with understanding and patience.
    c. Entertaining him/her with jokes to cheer him/her up.
    d. Giving him/her a precise and factual description of why he/she has a problem.

6. When I socialize, I prefer:
    a. Controlling the topics of conversation.
    b. Listening to others and validating their opinions.
    c. Being the life of the party.
    d. Staying in the background.

**PERSONALITY PROFILE – Continued**

7. When someone hurts me I tend to:
    a. Ignore it and move on.
    b. Feel deeply hurt.
    c. Laugh it off.
    d. Analyze why the person hurt me.

8. Friends see me as:
    a. Strong-willed.
    b. Nurturing and loving.
    c. Inspirational.
    d. Reserved.

9. I think of myself as more:
    a. Confident.
    b. Patient and tolerant.
    c. Laid back and easy going.
    d. A perfectionist.

10. I like:
    a. Adventure.
    b. Routine.
    c. Daring opportunities.
    d. Predictable situations.

11. When it comes to planning for a group, I get upset if:
    a. I'm not leading the planning session.
    b. There's a lot of conflict in the planning session.
    c. People don't allow for spontaneity or changes at the last minute.
    d. Others want to change the plans after they've been made.

12. In living with another person, it bothers me if he/she:
    a. Is not willing to take my suggestions.
    b. Is insensitive to my needs and feelings.
    c. Doesn't have a sense of humor.
    d. Is disorganized and leaves his/her things laying around.

13. My personality is more:
    a. Let's do it now.
    b. Adaptable.
    c. Easy going and laid back.
    d. Organized.

14. When it comes to work, I see myself as mostly:
    a. Productive.
    b. Giving and rational.
    c. Fun loving.
    d. Detailed.

**PERSONALITY PROFILE – Continued**

15. With other people, I'm good at:
    a. Leading.
    b. Listening.
    c. Motivating.
    d. Discerning.

16. In my spare time I tend to:
    a. Work on my goals.
    b. Do volunteer work.
    c. Be around other people.
    d. Read a non-fiction book.

17. When I have fifteen minutes to think by myself, I:
    a. Enjoy thinking about solving a challenge.
    b. Enjoy thinking about my friends and family.
    c. Dream about new ways to accomplish things.
    d. Think about working harder to perfect myself.

18. When others are in doubt about something, I like to:
    a. Do something just to get it done.
    b. Stay with things I know.
    c. Take a risk and try something new.
    d. Examine past procedures.

19. When something changes in my life, I generally:
    a. Adapt quickly and move on.
    b. Dislike it and have trouble adapting.
    c. Am enthusiastic and encourage others to accept change.
    d. Take time to learn the details in order to handle the change.

20. When there is conflict in my life, I generally:
    a. Act with confidence knowing I can solve it.
    b. Avoid any confrontation and hope for a peaceful resolution.
    c. Am optimistic and look for a creative solution.
    d. Investigate the source so I can take precise action.

## Instructions:

Add up your a's, b's, c's, and d's. The one that totals the highest is generally your dominant personality type. However, you may also have a high score in another area. This is normal. Many people are mixtures of several personality types. Review the descriptions that follow, especially the personality types in which you scored the highest, and then answer the questions relating to possible problems.

## TOTALS:

      **a's**_____          **b's**_____
      **c's**_____          **d's**_____

I have likened the four personality types to cars.

# a) ALL-TERRAIN VEHICLE
## This personality type likes to be a leader.

An All-Terrain Vehicle (ATV) is the "King of the Road" when it comes to motor vehicles operating on our highways today. It is ready to go into battle, lead a military maneuver, and stand up to any situation as leader of the pack. An ATV personality is determined in his/her goals. He/she is confident, independent, a self-starter, motivated, filled with courage and has the ability to rally others to his/her cause. This personality type will be your ardent defender and protector. On the downside, he/she may be controlling. At times this "in-charge" behavior can get in the way of compromise in a relationship.

# b) MINI VAN
## This personality type likes to help and serve others.

A Mini Van is a dependable car with the capabilities of being versatile and flexible.
A Mini Van personality type is loving, nurturing, and caring. He/she will drive many miles out of his/her way just to give a ride to the friendless. He/she will take chicken soup to a sick neighbor, take care of a friend's cat or dog, and field insults aimed at a friend and defend them out of loyalty. A Mini Van personality is tenderhearted and cries easily watching movies and reading books. He/she can be easily hurt because he/she tries so hard, loves so deeply, and gives so much. There is nothing half-hearted about anything the Mini Van decides to do or say. Mini Vans make the most dependable, loyal, and stable partners. On the downside, some Mini Vans do not like change. He/she might resist change and may make his/her mate uncomfortable when change occurs. In addition, others may take advantage of the giving nature of a Mini Van.

## c) SPORTS CAR
**This personality type needs to be liked, often is the life of the party, and loves to be creative.**

A Sports Car is the flashiest and most daring car on the road. In real life this personality can be equally flashy. This personality includes many of the entertainers and salesmen of the world. A Sports Car personality loves attention, adventure and new ways of doing things. He/she is often the one who comes up with the creative ideas in a group and loves a good party. It is not unusual to see the Sports Car the center of attention in most settings. This personality is fun loving, friendly to a fault, enthusiastic, and everybody's best friend. The downside to the Sports Car personality is that he/she might travel to his/her own timetable. Some Sports Car personality types don't like to make commitments or work to a schedule. The Sports Car type might agree to do something when pressured because they want to be liked, and then let you down and forget what he/she promised.

## d) EUROPEAN PRECISION CAR
**This personality type likes to be thorough and detailed.**

The European Precision Car personality type is detail oriented. He/she is thorough, exacting, accurate, steady, precise, a rule follower to the letter, dependable, organized to a fault, ten minutes early to every appointment, and good with money. The Precision Car will never just throw paint on a wall to get it done. He/she will spend weeks, if necessary, washing, stripping, and sanding the walls first. If you want any job done right, the Precision Car is the personality type to hire. Precision Car personality types are perfectionists. The downside to this personality is that he/she doesn't like to make decisions in a hurry, do anything fast just to get it done, or be spontaneous and adventurous without carefully thinking and planning it through.

# QUESTIONNAIRE #1

## HYBRID CAR PERSONALITY TYPES

**M**ost people are combinations of personality types just like there are hybrid cars. For example, you may be a combination of all car types, or just two. Look at your car types that have high numbers (generally 5 and above) and answer the three questions below and be honest. If you have trouble with this, ask a friend who knows you well.

1. List your car types with the most significant numbers:

2. Which traits from these car personality types do you have?

3. Which traits from these car personality types do you <u>not</u> have?

# STEP #1 – QUESTIONNAIRE #2

## QUESTIONS ON PERSONALITY CONFLICTS

**After reviewing your dominant personality types, answer the following questions for your types. Avoid the "three deadly issues": 1. Wanting too much to be liked, 2. Second guessing and 3. Manipulation. BE HONEST!**

**ALL-TERRAIN TYPES:**

1. If you are dominantly an All-Terrain type, do you think you might frustrate your partner with your ambition and drive? Has this been a problem for you previously?

2. If you are dominantly an All-Terrain type that is a workaholic, will your partner have scheduling conflicts with you because you are often unavailable? If so, list the obligations for your time that will affect your relationship?

3. If you are dominantly an All-Terrain type, would you possibly ignore issues that matter to your partner? Have you ever demeaned his/her ideas and concerns or considered them unimportant? List examples.

5. If you and your partner turn out to both be dominantly All-Terrain personality types, how will you deal with potential conflicts? How would you like to see your partner react when you come to a point where someone must be the leader and the other the follower?

STEP #1 – QUESTIONNAIRE # 2   **Continued**

## MINI-VAN TYPES:

1.  If you are dominantly a Mini-Van type personality, do you feel that your partner and others take advantage of your kindness and easy-going nature? What can you do about that?

2.  Having a Mini-Van personality, are you constantly helping with charities, church welfare and other service type projects? How will you deal with the situation if your partner doesn't accept your commitments?

3.  With a dominant Mini-Van personality, are you resistant to change? Will this be a problem if your partner constantly wants to try new things? How would you solve this?

4.  Sometimes a Mini-Van personality type appears to care more about other people than their partner. If this applies to you, how will you deal with this in your relationship?

## SPORTS CAR TYPES:

1.  If you are dominantly a Sports Car type and prefer a large circle of friends, and your partner does not, how will you compromise?

2.  If you are dominantly a Sports Car type and like to do things on the spur of the moment and your partner does not, how would you compromise if he/she objects?

3.  If you are dominantly a Sports Car type, are you habitually late or have you failed to follow through with a request made by your partner? Are these typical behaviors for you? If this is a problem for your partner, how can you resolve this in the future?

4. If you are dominantly a Sports Car type who is very outgoing, the life of the party and even boisterous at times, and your partner is shy and retiring, does this cause problems? If so, what could you do about it?

5. If you are a Sports Car type that generally doesn't worry about details, and your partner does, how will you deal with potential conflicts? Do you ever wish your partner would just "lighten up"? If they refuse to change, would that be a problem for you?

**PRECISION CAR TYPES:**

1. If you are dominantly a Precision Car type who is neat and tidy, and your partner is messy, will this be a problem? What could you do about it?

2. If you are a Precision Car type who prefers to stay at home and read a book rather than go out on the town, and your partner wants more of a social life, how would you compromise? List possible solutions.

3. If you are a Precision Car type who needs to have family planning sessions and your partner is more freewheeling, how will you deal with this? List solutions.

4. If you are a Precision Car type and put high importance on details, and your partner does not, will this be a problem? List solutions.

# QUESTIONNAIRES #1 AND #2
## CONCEPTS TO CONSIDER

A re you ignoring serious personality differences, thinking that they can be resolved after marriage? If so, remember that any needed changes or compromises should happen before an engagement and certainly a marriage. After a marriage, partners often secretly believe, "I've got him/her now. I don't have to change." Can you accept your partner just the way he/she is? Can you love him/her in spite of what you might consider to be serious flaws? If you are having any trouble in this area, how can you resolve it now? Is your partner willing to work with you? If not, this could be a warning sign that the two of you might be incompatible, and you should both seek professional counseling and/or consider ending the relationship.

*Fred was a Precision Car type personality, fastidious to a fault. His apartment looked like a set for the magazine "Better Homes and Gardens." If anyone touched an item in his apartment, he would remove it from the offender's hand, and put it back in the exact location it was positioned previously. His biggest pet peeve in life was "things out of place." Furthermore, he was always ten minutes early to every appointment. He detested being late. It caused him enormous anxiety.*

*Jamie, Fred's fiancée, was messy to a fault. She never remembered where she put things. She would periodically try to organize her apartment and then forget her reasoning behind the plan. Water glasses would drift into the cupboard filled with plates and cooking pans would end up in the drawers designated for mixing bowls. Almost every day it was a ritual to find her keys. Fred tried helping her. First, he gave her a key finder. Clap twice and the key ring would make a noise. This cut down on the time for finding her keys but didn't solve the rest of the problems that invaded every aspect of Jamie's life. She was always thirty minutes late. Her friends just knew that about her and accepted it. But now after six months together, it was wearing on Fred's nerves. What could he do? He was desperately in love with Jamie. She was charming, captivating, and the most beautiful woman he had ever known. And she loved him and wanted to marry him! Could he live with her flaws? Or would these irritating habits eventually drive them apart?*

*They decided to get engaged and marry without resolving their differences. At first, the marriage went well, but soon the problems resurfaced. They started to have loud disagreements. Accusations about unwillingness to change or compromise increased. They started professional counseling. Nothing positive resulted at first. Fred couldn't stand her habitual tardiness. He resented cleaning up the apartment after her. Finally, he moved out. Fortunately, they continued counseling. Because their desire to save the marriage was so strong, they began to see that both compromise and change were necessary. With the help of a counselor, they developed a plan. Jamie agreed to set her clocks one half hour ahead so she would arrive at appointments on time. Fred resolved to rearrange things in the house periodically and to label shelves so that items tended to return to their proper place. A climate of tolerance for each other's faults and gratitude for strengths was developed. Without the help of a gifted counselor, they probably would have divorced. Imagine how much better it would have been if they had resolved these issues before the engagement and marriage.*

**" A person who marries with the intent of changing his/her spouse later is doomed at minimum to pain and difficulty, and at maximum divorce."**

# STEP #1– QUESTIONNAIRE #3

## ACTIVITIES

List the activities you currently pursue and plan on doing when you are engaged and married. Examples: football, baseball, basketball, soccer, computer games, TV, clubs, hobbies, camping, hiking, biking, golf, horseback riding, hunting, shopping, tennis, dance, etc.

| ACTIVITY | HOW OFTEN (Daily, Weekly, Monthly) | TIME SPENT (Estimated) |
|---|---|---|
| 1. | | |
| 2. | | |
| 3. | | |
| 4. | | |
| 5. | | |
| 6. | | |
| 7. | | |
| 8. | | |
| 9. | | |
| 10. | | |

CONCEPTS TO CONSIDER

# QUESTIONNAIRE #3

Now that you've done an analysis regarding your favorite activities, it's important to take some time and think about what happens when there's another significant person in your life. Do you foresee problems in your future marriage regarding your activities? For example, if one of you is passionate about horses and the other one is allergic to animals, you may have a problem. Are there activities that you refuse to support after you have a family such as motorcycle riding, mountain climbing or skydiving? When you get together to discuss this section of Step #1, take some time to discuss where there might be conflicts. Go over each activity that you want to continue and discuss your partner's view. Is your partner willing to participate in activities you love? Discuss the level of importance of this part of your life and see if you need to compromise. If you become disappointed in his/her attitude about an important activity, you may want to slow down your relationship until you find resolution – either through open and honest discussion or professional counseling. If you find resolution impossible, the only answer may be that you break up and look for a person with whom you have more in common.

*A couple with three children wished that they had never married. The husband was passionate about rock climbing. His wife knew about his love of the sport before they married. She assumed that he would quit after the wedding. He assumed that he would continue and that she would support him. They never discussed it prior to marriage. The wife detested the time her husband spent away from their family. She also resented the money he spent on rock climbing rather than on family activities that they all could share. Money was tight and neither of them could come to a compromise. They refused to listen to any advice and finally ended their relationship in divorce, a very painful time for their children. This mistake would now hurt many generations to come because they failed to do their homework prior to the engagement and wedding.*

# STEP #1 QUESTIONNAIRE #4
## WHO ARE YOU AND WHAT ARE YOUR EXPECTATIONS?

**DIRECTIONS:**
1. Go through the lists below and **circle** your likes, values, qualities, and accomplishments.
2. Go through the list again and put a **check mark** by the qualities you think your partner has.
3. Next, go through the list again and put a **plus sign** by what you want and need in a partner. Add in any qualities that are not listed but are essential to you.

## VALUES/QUALITIES

| | | |
|---|---|---|
| Humble/teachable | Adventurous | Flexible |
| Ambitious | Thinks outside the box | Open-minded |
| Sense of humor | Rule follower | Reliable |
| Spiritual | Thrifty | Charming |
| Leader | Happy go-lucky | Animal lover |
| Easy going | Confident | Outdoorsy |
| Intelligent | Loyal | Athletic |
| Intellectual | Appreciative | Service minded |
| Hard worker | Seeks knowledge | Spontaneous |
| Serious–minded | Courageous | Team Player |
| Positive | Self-disciplined | Likes children |
| Honest | Virtuous | Has manners, knows etiquette |
| Kind and loving | Affectionate | Values the environment |
| Generous | Articulate | |
| Sensitive to others | Creative | |
| Charitable | High energy | |

Other_____##_____

## ACCOMPLISHMENTS/TALENTS
Has a college education
Has completed training in a trade
Has an advanced degree
Has knowledge/training to fix cars
Has knowledge/training to repair household issues
Has knowledge/training to do carpentry work
Has domestic skills: cooking and sewing
Has ability to paint inside/outside house
Is musical, plays an instrument
Is cultured
Is scientific
Has a profession and career plan
Has a job
Deeply spiritual/committed to his/her religion
Other_____

STEP #1 – QUESTIONNAIRE #4 - Continued

## ACTIVITIES

Charity work
Theatre/plays
Ballet /Opera performances
Art museums
Science museums
Sporting events: baseball, football, and
basketball games
Watching sports regularly on TV
Participate on sports teams together
Watching TV mystery/police programs
Watching love story movies
Watching action/adventure movies
Hiking
Biking
Traveling
Golfing

Playing chess
Playing video games
Playing tennis
Reading
Political activities
Weekly religious/spiritual activities
Shopping
Hunting
Fishing
Camping
Boating
Horseback riding
Exercising at a club
Dancing
Other_____

_____

## POLITICS
Democrat
Republican
Independent

Pacifist
Socialist
Neutral/don't really care

## SEXUAL & RELATIONSHIP EXPERIENCE
Has never been married previously.
Has been previously married and divorced.
Has been married and spouse died.
Has never lived with someone outside of marriage.
Has lived with partners.
Has had less than 10 sexual partners.
Has had less than 20 sexual partners.
Is free of any and all STD's.
Doesn't matter

## WHAT MY PARTNER MUST FEEL ABOUT ME, MY FRIENDS & FAMILY

Thinks I'm attractive to him/her "as is."
Concentrates on me when we are together, without texting or emailing, or looking around at other people.
Is interested in what I do for work and hobbies.
Is willing to help me when I need help.
Is willing to be social with my friends and family when I want to be.

**STEP #1 – QUESTIONNAIRE #4 Continued**

## <u>WHAT IS CRITICAL AND NON-NEGOTIABLE</u>?: Check each one that is applicable.

- o No drug addictions
- o Does not look at nor is addicted to pornography
- o Doesn't smoke
- o Doesn't drink alcohol
- o Doesn't gamble
- o Not addicted to Video games
- o Not addicted to shopping
- o Not addicted to food for comfort
- o Not addicted to caffeinated drinks of any kind
- o Has no mental illnesses such as Bi-Poplar, Serious Depression, Anxiety, Borderline Personality disorder, Narcissistic Personality Disorder etc.
- o Has no chronic physical illnesses
- o Other_____

## REVIEW:

Compare your lists. Are your circled items different from the ones checked for your partner? Are the check marks different from the plus signs? Does it appear that you both have the same likes, similar experiences and preferences? For example, does your partner spend hours watching sports on TV and you don't share his/her passion? Is this difference serious enough to jeopardize a great relationship? If so, could it cause the two of you to eventually drift apart? Are there other areas of concern?

# STEP #1 — QUESTIONNAIRE #5
## WHAT ARE YOUR DREAMS/GOALS ABOUT A FUTURE MARRIAGE?

List twelve or more dreams you have about a future marriage. (Examples: vacation to Europe, children, a dog, weekly date, being greeted with a hug and kiss from your partner, intimacy every night, no arguing, specific car preference, dream home, financial expectations, desire to have a bohemian lifestyle, live on little income, only work when necessary, a farm with fruit trees, chickens, cows, and vegetable garden, live in a log cabin in Alaska, live in a foreign country, live in a penthouse in NYC, own a vacation home, career goals and more, etc.)

1. _____
2. _____
3. _____
4. _____
5. _____
6. _____
7. _____
8. _____
9. _____
10. _____
11. _____
12. _____
13. _____
14. _____
15. _____
16. _____

During your activities, lunch and afternoon, discuss whether each of you would be willing to try to make the other's dreams come true by talking about how each will help the other. Are some of your partner's dreams unimportant or unacceptable to either of you? Why? Will this be a problem in the future?

# STEP #1 — QUESTIONNAIRE #6
## WHAT ARE YOUR EXPECTATIONS FOR THE ROLES YOUR PARNTER SHOULD PLAY IN YOUR RELATIONSHIP?

List specific expectations you have for the roles your partner should play in a marriage. (Examples: traditional roles such as the wife cooks the meals, does the laundry, the husband does repairs, mows the lawn and is solely responsible for earning the living. Or modern roles: the wife works full time earning half the living and they share the duties of cooking, cleaning, and changing future baby diapers. Or do you expect your husband or wife to fulfill the same roles as your mother and father?)

1._____

2._____

3._____

4._____

5._____

6._____

7._____

8._____

9._____

10._____

11._____

12._____

13._____

14._____

15._____

16._____

During your discussions, read your lists to each other and discuss what each will or will not do to fulfill these expectations. Identify problem areas and philosophical differences. Then decide how you could solve these issues. Is your partner willing to compromise?

# STEP #1 – QUESTIONNAIRE #7

## DREAMS & EXPECTATIONS FOR THE HOLIDAYS & GIFT GIVING

1. Describe your expectations and dreams for celebrating holidays with your partner such as Christmas, Easter, Thanksgiving, Hanukah, and others.

2. List holiday traditions you can't live without each year.

3. Are any of your holiday plans based on an obligation to friends or family? If so, how would you handle this when you're married?

4. What are your expectations for gifts on birthdays, anniversaries, Christmas, etc.?

5. For whom should you buy presents, besides each other, on holidays? What are your expectations for gift exchanges?

6. Do you believe in going into debt to buy gifts?

7. Do you prefer gifts to be a total surprise? Or, do you prefer to know about them, maybe even help pick them out, and then have them given to you as a "surprise."?

8. How would you handle it if your partner gives you a present you do not like? Should you pretend you like it? What about cost issues, if the gift was expensive?

# STEP #1 – QUESTIONNAIRE #8
## CHILDREN AND YOUR EXPECTATIONS

1.  Do you want to have children when you're married, and how many children do you want? Who should have the final say on whether to have more children?

2.  How soon after marriage would you want to have children?

3.  Do you believe in birth control? What kind? Should it be the woman's or the man's responsibility? Are you worried about possible negative health consequences from taking hormone birth control pills?

4.  If your partner does not want to have children and you do, are you willing to give up your preference?

5.  Do you think that there is an ideal spacing in years between children?

6.  If you have a Down syndrome or special needs child, what is your philosophy on how to cope? What are your thoughts about abortion if you know a child will be born with mental issues or deformities?

7.  What are your beliefs about the roles a husband/wife should have in rearing children? Is it mostly the Mother's role or is it equally shared?

8.  Do you believe in having a set of rules for your children to follow at the various stages of their lives? If so, what are some of the specifics?

9. What are your thoughts on disciplining children?

10. Do you agree with the way your parents disciplined you? What would you change?

11. What are key elements in good parenting?

12. Are you a "letter-of-the-law (rules) person" or a "spirit-of-the-law person" when it comes to rearing children? Do you expect your partner to agree with your philosophy?

13. Should children have chores and at what age should they start? Should children be paid for chores around the house?

14. What do you think about holding special weekly family get-togethers such as: playing sports together, having a game night, or movie night with the family, etc.?

15. How do you feel about bedtimes for children?

16. How should children be treated when they are sick?

17. What are the most important values that you would teach your children?

# QUESTIONNAIRE #8
## CONCEPTS TO CONSIDER

Does your partner want children and you absolutely do not? If you are not united when it comes to this issue, perhaps you should seek a mate who has the same expectations? Think carefully. Unless conflicts about having children are resolved, you will most certainly experience heartache after marriage.

*Juliet married Larry in spite of the knowledge that he did not want children, and warnings from her best friend. She was convinced that she could change his mind. Discussions about children drove them further apart. After ten years of marriage, nothing had changed. Juliet loved Larry but felt a profound emptiness because of his unwillingness to have children. Juliet regretted not listening to the voice of wisdom prior to the wedding.*

**DO NOT FALL INTO THIS TRAP:** "I can change him/her after we're married."

What are your philosophies on rearing children? Are they radically different from those of your partner? Are you able to compromise? Would your partner consider taking a class on parenting skills and techniques? If that's important to you, get a commitment! Perhaps you should take a short parenting course now to see if you can work together on such an important subject.

*Carol came from parents who were disciplinarians. Isaac came from ex-hippie parents that had no rules. They could foresee parenting disputes, so they decided to take a community college night school class on parenting. It was a success for them. Together they read, discussed, and formulated a parenting style that they both embraced. After marriage and two children, they were proud to report that they had peace, harmony, and love in their home, thanks to the work they did prior to their marriage.*

**REMEMBER: You can conceivably fall in love with several different men or women. Falling in love does not necessarily mean that you are well suited for each other for a lifetime of marriage. Being united is critical for a successful relationship to last the test of time.**

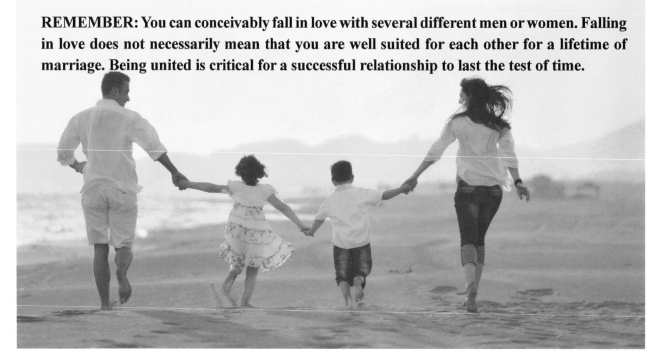

# STEP #1

## MORE CONCEPTS TO CONSIDER

I had the privilege of meeting a couple that had been married for thirty years. They were still deeply in love with each other. I asked them the secret to their success. The woman said that it was all in the selection process. In fact, she had almost married another man. I was surprised and asked her what made her change her mind. She readily revealed the following story.

*Marta had fallen in love with Phil during her freshman year of college and they continued to date each other for four years. Upon graduation, both accepted job offers in different areas of the country, he in Alaska and she in Chicago. After only a month of separation, they missed each other dreadfully. So, they scheduled a romantic vacation for September. It was a bicycle tour of France. At the end of the trip Phil proposed marriage and she agreed. They were deeply in love, and the romantic bicycle trip convinced them both that they were meant for each other. After he returned to his job in Alaska and she returned to her work in Chicago, they began to converse via phone and e-mail. Within one month they discovered that their dreams, expectations of marriage, and life goals were vastly different. She wanted to stay and live in the big city. He wanted to live in the back woods of Alaska. She wanted to attend plays, the ballet, and sophisticated parties. He wanted to hunt, fish, and watch TV at home in the evening. She wanted to plan charity events and write poetry. His idea of a dream home was a log cabin in the woods. Her idea of a dream home was a penthouse in the city. She tried a week in Alaska, and he tried a week in Chicago. After the experience, it was clear that neither wanted the same things in marriage. They decided to break up. She cried and cried. Not only was she still in love with Phil, she had invested four years of her life dating him.*

*"What gave you the courage to call off the engagement?" I asked Marta.*

*"I realized that our expectations and dreams of marriage were so different. I knew that we would both be frustrated in marriage and eventually end in divorce. He agreed. A year later he met a wonderful girl in Alaska, a forestry ranger who loved to hunt and fish. I met a young aspiring lawyer who loved to attend the theater. Today Phil is still married and so am I. We still send cards at Christmas and are so thankful that we didn't make a mistake in marrying each other. It didn't mean that we weren't terrific partners. We were, but just not for each other. Thank heavens we both had the good sense to realize that love alone would not make a good marriage."*

**PONDER:**

At the end of your discussion with your partner, make sure you try to come to an agreement or compromise on any issues with which you differed. The purpose of all these exercises is to bring out into the open, all the issues that might cause conflict within a relationship. Are you right for each other? Do you both want to help make each other's dreams come true? Alone that evening, write down your thoughts and feelings in the Journal for Step #1 at the end of the book. If you feel good about your progress, you're ready for Step #2.

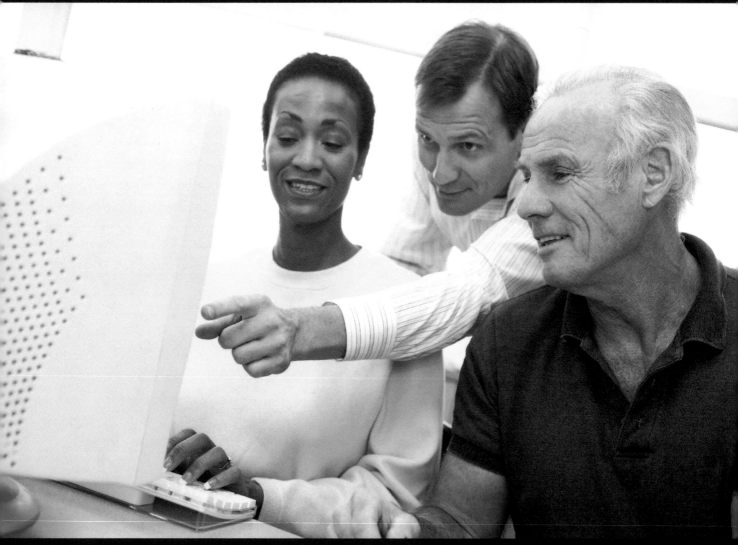

# STEP #2
# HOW ARE YOUR PEOPLE SKILLS?

## INTRODUCTION

It's critical in any relationship that you have good people skills. There are a few among us who have these naturally. Most of us, however, have to learn how to listen, how to communicate ideas, feelings and concerns, how to work with others, how to compromise, how to resolve conflicts, and how to make a relationship strong and healthy for all involved. In order to have a wonderful connection with others, learning the skills to relate well requires practice. In this step, we take you through the process. It's important to follow each part, even if it seems simplistic at first. Reading is not enough. Being humble and knowing that you learn by doing is important. As you make the simple principles from this step into habits, you will see how well they work. Some people think that just because they can talk and make whole sentences, that they are good communicators. Nothing could be further from the truth. In my years as a therapist, I have found that the best success in relationships comes when each person involved is willing to humble him or herself to start with communication basics and build and practice until the principles and skills come naturally. This step will give you what you need to make sure your relationship is one you want to continue for the rest of your life. Relax and enjoy the process.

# STEP #2
## INSTRUCTIONS

**a.  Preparation:**

    a.  Separately, read the entire step and fill out questionnaire #1.

**b.  Plan:**

    a.  Review the Babysitting Assignment/Guidelines. Arrange with a family to do babysitting and select an evening with your partner (*probably a Friday*).

    b.  Schedule the next morning together (*probably a Saturday*), and pick a place to clean, such as your and/or your partner's apartment/house. Use the chore list.

    c.  Schedule a place for that same afternoon and evening to spend together to practice the conflict resolution and art of compromise exercises.

    d.  Plan meals as they fit into your schedule.

**c.  Activity:**

    a.  Perform the babysitting together as outlined. After the babysitting is over, each of you go home and fill out questionnaire #2 alone.

    b.  The next morning, do the cleaning as planned and note how you relate. Afterward, take a break from each other and fill out questionnaire #3.

    c.  After lunch, use the conflicts noted while babysitting and/or cleaning to practice the conflict resolution exercises. If no conflicts were identified, use ones from other disagreements or make up some for practice.

    d.  Take a break between each exercise and go for a walk together to talk and discuss your reactions and feelings.

    e.  Study the Art of Compromise together. Then do the exercises.

    f.  Do your best to make this fun. Relax and enjoy being together.

**d.  AFTER:**

    a.  Fill out questionnaire #4 by yourself at home.

    b.  Record in your journal at the end of the book, your feelings about your abilities to communicate with each other and solve problems.

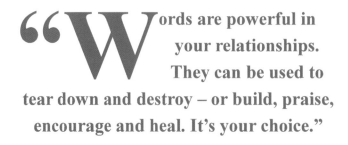

"**W**ords are powerful in your relationships. They can be used to tear down and destroy – or build, praise, encourage and heal. It's your choice."

# STEP #2 – QUESTIONNAIRE #1
## COMMUNICATION SKILLS AND PROBLEM SOLVING

1. Have you had a disagreement with your partner? How was it solved? Were you satisfied with the solution?

2. Are you avoiding talk about any issue at this time? If so, why haven't you been able to talk about it?

3. Are you able to tell your partner what you think at any given time? Or are you afraid to talk to your partner for fear that he/she will get upset?

4. Does your partner stop talking to you when he/she gets mad? Does he/she walk away in such situations thereby avoiding a solution to the problem? If so, describe.

5. How do you let your partner know when you're angry? How does he/she react?

6. How do you wish your partner would talk to you when he/she is angry, mad, upset, or unhappy with something you've said or done?

7. Does your partner ever get jealous and try to control you in any way?

8. Does your partner become defensive when you discuss problems?

9. Does your partner ever ridicule you privately or in public? Does your partner put you down or make you the butt of jokes? If so, describe.

10. Is your partner the type who always has to be right? Does he/she always have the last word? Do you sometimes feel like he/she wants to control your every thought and move? If so, describe.

11. How do you differ with your partner in the ways you express yourself to each other?

12. What areas do you think are communication problems in your relationship?

# STEP #2
## BABYSITTING ASSIGNMENT / GUIDELINES

Arrange for a babysitting assignment for you and your partner. This is best early on a Friday evening. Pick a family that has some toddlers and older children. A small baby is probably too much. One child is too easy. Hopefully one of you has some experience. Here are a few guidelines:

Babysitting can be a dangerous job if you don't lay down the law and follow the parents' wishes. Here are a few guidelines to follow:

1. Make the children pick up after themselves. No mess when the parents return.
2. Stop unruly behavior early before it gets out of hand.
3. Be wary of children saying, "Our mom lets us do it!" She might, but probably not.
4. Don't let other children come over unless arranged with the parents.
5. Don't let the children go to a neighbor's house unless it's all pre-arranged.
6. Don't let them play video games and watch TV all the time. Switch up activities.
7. Honor the bedtime the parents give. It's unfair to the children to let them stay up late.
8. Make sure the children know you follow the rules.
9. Don't have any friends of yours come over while babysitting.
10. Don't drink alcohol even if the parents allow it.
11. Stay off the phone except to talk to the parents.
12. Don't take the children on excursions unless the parents approve.
13. Don't let the children disappear in their rooms longer than 15 minutes. Check on them regularly and don't let them lock the doors.
14. In an emergency, call 911 and then the parents. Have their cell numbers.
15. Don't watch questionable movies while babysitting
16. Watch your mouth. Don't curse.
17. Don't post or tag any photos of the children. This is just not done.
18. When in doubt, call the parents for help immediately.
19. No physical discipline. It's not your job or right.
20. Don't give a bath unless you're supposed to and you have experience. Better not.
21. Keep play gentle.
22. Stay alert to everything that's happening. Quiet doesn't necessarily mean everything's OK.

This activity is to see how you both work with children and with each other. You should plan activities for the children possibly including the following:

1. Read them stories
2. Play some games: "hide and seek," board games, simple puzzle, singing songs, charades.
3. Play catch with a ball.
4. Make cookies if approved by parents.

Observe each other's behavior and note any conflicts you have between the two of you. With children it's probably inevitable. Save the conflict resolution until after the children are in bed.

# STEP #2 – QUESTIONNAIRE #2
## WORKING WITH CHILDREN
(fill out alone after babysitting)

1. While babysitting together, did you have any conflicts or disagreements? If so, list them.

2. How were you and your partner in being creative with the children?

3. Were there things that the children did that bothered you or your partner? If so, did you find solutions and what were they?

4. Did you or your partner become visibly angered at one or more of the children? What resulted?

5. Did you or your partner have any problem with the children picking up after themselves? If so, what do you think was the reason for their behavior?

6. Did you or your partner deviate from any of the guidelines given on the previous page? If so, how and why? Explain.

7. During the evening, did you have to call the parents? If so, how was that decision made and what was the result?

8. Did the children have arguments with each other? If so, how did you and your partner handle the conflict?

9.  Did your partner participate in activities with the children? How well did he/she do with them?

10. At any time during the evening, did you feel that you ended up doing most of the work? Or was it the opposite? If so, why do you think it happened that way?

11. Did the children say a prayer before they went to bed? If so, were you and your partner comfortable joining with them? If you have your own children, would you expect them to say prayers, study religious ideas and attend church? If so, what religion?

12. Were you asked to help any of the children with homework? If you have your own children, how would you handle their education? Would public schools be OK for your children, or would you want to send them to a private or religious school or home school them?

13. After seeing these children interact and considering your own values, would you allow your children to have cell phones, play video games and have access to social networking?

# STEP #2
## CLEANING ASSIGNMENT

**The next morning after babysitting, plan to do some cleaning together at your or your partner's apartment/house.**

### DIVIDE UP AND DECIDE WHO DOES WHAT CHORES

**HOUSEHOLD CHORES:** *Circle the ones you will do and check those for your partner.*

**Living Room**

1. Vacuum the carpet
2. Dust
3. Tidy up
4. Other

**Bathrooms**

1. Clean the toilet
2. Clean the sink
3. Clean the bathtub
4. Clean the shower
5. Sweep and mop the floor
6. Other

**Bedrooms**

1. Change the sheets on the bed(s),wash them, and remake the bed.
2. Vacuum
3. Dust
4. Other

**Kitchen**

1. Wash any dirty dishes and clean the sink
2. Clean the counters
3. Sweep and mop the floor

Add any other rooms/spaces that need to be cleaned.

# STEP #2 – QUESTIONNAIRE #3
## (fill out alone after cleaning)

1. While cleaning together, did you have any conflicts or disagreements? If so, list them.

2. Did the chore plan work? Was your partner cooperative in that regard?

3. Were you efficient in the process? Did either of you prefer to talk rather than work?

4. Did you discover any sensitivities to chemicals or other cleaning compounds for either of you?

5. Did you feel you worked harder than your partner? If so, did that bother you?

6. Did you or your partner boss the other one around? Did one take the role of leader without consulting the other?

7. Did you have any experiences where you had to make a compromise? If so, how did that go?

# CONFLICT RESOLUTION

## STEP # 2
### CONFLICT RESOLUTION ASSIGNMENT

After babysitting and cleaning, read the guidelines and format for conflict resolution <u>out loud</u> together. Then practice the exercises, dividing your roles into **The Presenter**, the partner who brings up the conflict for discussion, and **The Listener**, the partner to whom the conflict is explained. Practice the exercises by staying with one role through resolution. Then reverse the roles so you learn both sides of the process.

<u>Presenter Guidelines:</u>
1. **Set the tone** with a compliment. Example: "You are wonderful to be willing to talk about this."

2. **Let your partner off the hook** to start the conflict/resolution process. Example: "I know you didn't mean to hurt me just then. You were probably preoccupied." Letting him/her off the hook will immediately remove or at least reduce a defensive attitude.

3. **Use "I" statements** in presenting the problem. For example: "I feel hurt when you make fun of me in front of others." Avoid blaming statements and words such as "you always" and "you never." Only speak about the present issue. Do **not** say things such as, "You are <u>always</u> so hurtful to me," or "You <u>never</u> pick up after yourself." Instead, address only the issue at hand using "I" statements: "I felt like I was your butler when I had to carry your bag of golf clubs, bag of sports clothes, and all the food out to the car, and you didn't try to help."

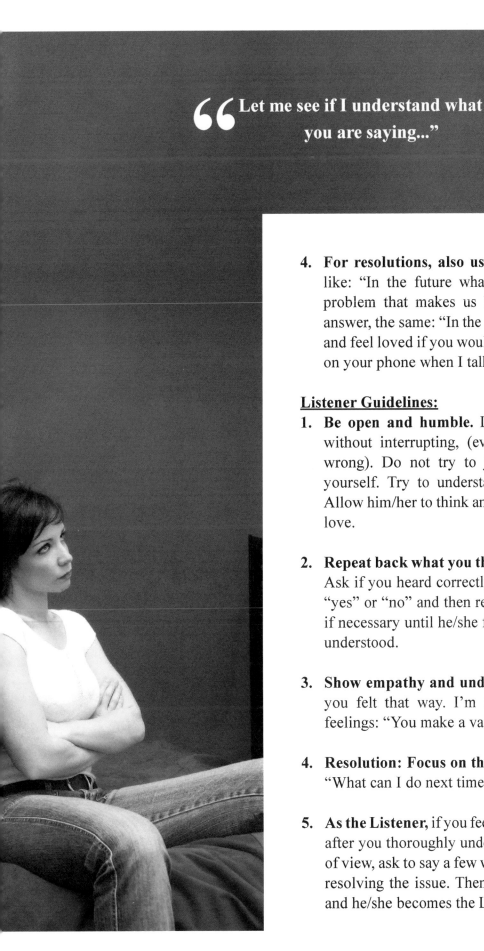

> **Let me see if I understand what you are saying..."**

4. **For resolutions, also use "I" or "we" statements** like: "In the future what can **we** do to solve this problem that makes us both happy?" And for the answer, the same: "In the future **I** would really love it and feel loved if you would stop looking at your texts on your phone when I talk to you."

**Listener Guidelines:**

1. **Be open and humble.** Listen to his/her complaint without interrupting, (even if you think he/she is wrong). Do not try to justify yourself or defend yourself. Try to understand his/her point of view. Allow him/her to think and feel, showing respect and love.

2. **Repeat back what you think the other person said.** Ask if you heard correctly. Give him/her time to say "yes" or "no" and then repeat and reflect back again if necessary until he/she feels satisfied that you have understood.

3. **Show empathy and understanding:** "I had no idea you felt that way. I'm so sorry." Validate his/her feelings: "You make a valid point."

4. **Resolution: Focus on the goal to resolve the issue.** "What can I do next time to make you happy?"

5. **As the Listener,** if you feel a need to explain yourself, after you thoroughly understand your partner's point of view, ask to say a few words in your behalf prior to resolving the issue. Then you become the Presenter and he/she becomes the Listener.

# STEP # 2
## CONFLICT RESOLUTION ASSIGNMENT

**GENERAL GUIDELINES:**

1. No screaming, yelling, swearing, name-calling, criticizing, belittling, or making fun of your partner's viewpoint. Allow your partner to have his/her feelings.

2. Do not get mad, angry, withdraw or walk away refusing to resolve a conflict. Refusal to listen and resolve is a slap in the face to your partner. It is the same as if you said, "I don't love you enough to listen to your feelings. I don't love you enough to value your feelings and resolve them." Bite your tongue. Stop thinking about yourself and listen. Stick it out. The result will be worth the effort.

3. IF THERE IS A SEVERE ANGER PROBLEM: 1. Make the sports hand "T" sign for Time Out, 2. Say, "I care about this and will return in 30 minutes when I have calmed down." 3. Run around the block, beat on a boxing bag, go to the gym, meditate, take deep breaths or use any other techniques that help you release your anger. Then return with anger subdued and under control to resolve the conflict.

4. Have faith in the process. Regard the process as an opportunity to become closer to your partner and deepen your relationship. Then it will be a WIN/WIN.

## FORMAT FOR CONFLICT RESOLUTION
### EXAMPLE OF HOW IT SHOULD WORK:

### *Setting the tone*

**PRESENTER**: "Thank you for caring about me and our relationship. I really appreciate your willingness to resolve the issue that is bothering me."

**LISTENER:** "Of course. I love you and want to do whatever it takes. So, go ahead and tell me what is bothering you."

### *Letting them off the hook*

**PRESENTER:** "Okay. Well, I know you didn't mean to hurt me today when we were cleaning my apartment. But I felt really upset when I was cleaning the bathroom and you came in to see how I was doing, and you told me that I was doing it wrong. Then you said that you'd have to reclean the whole bathroom with a disinfectant cleanser with bleach because I was using an ineffective natural product that didn't sterilize the bathroom fixtures."

## *Repeating back*

**LISTENER:** "So you didn't like it that I criticized you for using a natural cleaning product when I prefer to use a household cleaner that I feel sterilizes the bathroom."

**PRESENTER:** "Yes, that's how I feel. I've been cleaning my bathroom just fine with natural cleaning products for many years and it worked just fine."

## *Restating for understanding*

**LISTENER**: "Let me see if I understand you. You feel that it is okay to clean your bathroom with natural products. In fact, you have done it for many years and find it offensive that I would question your cleaning strategies."

**PRESENTER:** Yes. You got it.

## *Empathy and willingness to change*

**LISTENER:** "I'm so sorry. What can I do to solve this? What do you need me to do in the future?"

**PRESENTER:** "How about this? Let's compromise. Whenever I'm in charge of cleaning the bathroom, I do it my way with no criticism and when you're in charge, you clean it your way and use whatever cleaning products you want, and I won't criticize you. Since we will probably never agree on the same way to do this, we'll just determine the process by who is in charge at the time. Are you willing to do that?"

## *Resolution*

**LISTENER:** "Yes. No problem. I can do that. It's a great plan."

**PRESENTER:** "Thanks for listening and resolving this with me. I feel great now. You're the best."

### BAD EXAMPLE OF CONFLICT RESOLUTION SESSION

**PRESENTER:** "You really hurt me when you said you'd have to reclean the bathroom."

**LISTENER:** "Oh, come on. You know I'm right..."

**PRESENTER**: "Why are you being so insensitive?"

**LISTENER:** "Get over it. You're the sensitive one. In fact, you're too sensitive. Lighten up." (And then the partner walks away refusing to listen and resolve the issue.)

# EXERCISES FOR PRACTICING CONFLICT RESOLUTION

## PRACTICE INSTRUCTIONS #1:

Select an unresolved issue from babysitting, house cleaning or something else in your relationship. Use the conflict resolution guidelines. Make sure that you both understand them completely and agree to abide by them. If, for some reason, you cannot find an issue to resolve, make one up and role-play the exercise.

## FILL IN YOUR OWN PROBLEM/ISSUE USING THE FOLLOWING FORMAT

### *Setting the tone*

**PRESENTER**: "I'm really grateful for our friendship. You really make me happy when you listen to me."

**LISTENER**: "I feel the same. What's up?"

### *Letting them off the hook*

**PRESENTER:** "It isn't like you to hurt my feelings, but something happened today."

**LISTENER:** "I'm sorry. What did I do?"

### *Presenting and repeating back*

**PRESENTER:** "Well, today I really felt hurt when you _____."

**LISTENER**: "Let me see if I understand what you are saying. You felt hurt when I _____
_____. Is that right?"

**PRESENTER:** "Almost, but not quite. I felt that_____."

**LISTENER:** "You mean that_____."

**PRESENTER:** "Yes, exactly."

### *Demonstration of Empathy*

**LISTENER**: "Wow. I had no idea that you felt that way. I'm so sorry. I never meant to hurt you or make you feel badly or resentful of me. That's the last thing I want in our relationship. Please forgive me."

**PRESENTER:** "Of course, I forgive you. I appreciate your sensitivity and willingness to make our relationship work."

## *Willingness to solve the problem*

**LISTENER:** "What can I do next time to make this work for us? I want to make it better."

**PRESENTER:** "What I really want is for you to_____. That would make me feel good about us."

## *Resolution*

**LISTENER:** "Okay, I can do that. Next time this situation occurs, I will _____ _____."

**PRESENTER:** "That's great. You understood me well."

## *The Guarantee*

**LISTENER:** "But just in case I slip up sometime again, could you just give me a gentle reminder, like a code word such as 'Danger zone' or 'Ouch!' It would jog my memory and give me a chance to make it right. Eventually I'll make it a habit."

**PRESENTER:** "'Ouch' it is. That's a great idea. Thanks. I love you so much."

**LISTENER:** "I love you too."

## NOTE:

This form is not cast in concrete. But, stay with it closely until you can do it easily. Then you can play with it if it's more comfortable with some changes. Remember the elements are:

1. Setting the tone
2. Letting the other person off the hook
3. Presenting and repeating back
4. Demonstrating empathy
5. Willingness to solve the problem
6. Resolution
7. And a guarantee if you need it

If you find that you are having serious problems communicating and your partner is not willing to resolve conflicts with you according to this pattern for effective conflict resolution, and you want to continue the relationship, seek a professional counselor.

## PRACTICE INSTRUCTIONS #2:

Now reverse the roles. If you were the Listener, now role-play the Presenter and vice versa for your partner. Again, select an unresolved issue from babysitting, house cleaning or something else in your relationship. Use the conflict resolution guidelines. Make sure that you both understand them completely and agree to abide by them. If, for some reason, you cannot find an issue to resolve, make one up and role-play the exercise.

## FILL IN YOUR OWN PROBLEM/ISSUE USING THE FOLLOWING FORMAT

### *Setting the tone*

**PRESENTER**: "I'm really grateful for our friendship. You really make me happy when you listen to me."

**LISTENER**: "I feel the same. What's up?"

### *Letting them off the hook*

**PRESENTER:** "It isn't like you to hurt my feelings, but something happened today."

**LISTENER:** "I'm sorry. What did I do?"

### *Presenting and repeating back*

**PRESENTER:** "Well, today I really felt hurt when you _____."

**LISTENER:** "Let me see if I understand what you are saying. You felt hurt when I _____ _____ . Is that right?"

**PRESENTER:** "Almost, but not quite. I felt that_____."

**LISTENER:** "You mean that_____."

**PRESENTER**: "Yes, exactly."

### *Demonstration of Empathy*

**LISTENER**: "Wow. I had no idea that you felt that way. I'm so sorry. I never meant to hurt you or make you feel badly or resentful of me. That's the last thing I want in our relationship. Please forgive me."

**PRESENTER:** "Of course, I forgive you. I appreciate your sensitivity and willingness to make our relationship work."

## *Willingness to solve the problem*

**LISTENER:** "What can I do next time to make this work for us?"

**PRESENTER:** "What I really want is for you to_____.
That would make me feel good about us."

## *Resolution*

**LISTENER:** "Okay, I can do that. Next time this situation occurs, I will _____
_____."

**PRESENTER:** "That's great. You understood me well."

## *The Guarantee*

**LISTENER:** "But just in case I slip up sometime again, could you just give me a gentle reminder, like a code word such as 'Danger zone' or 'Ouch!' It would jog my memory and give me a chance to make it right. Eventually I'll make it a habit."

**PRESENTER**: "'Ouch' it is. That's a great idea. Thanks. I love you so much."

**LISTENER:** "I love you too."

Practice this format as often as you need until it comes naturally. I can't emphasize the importance of this enough. We all have patterns on how we deal with each other. Most of us have developed patterns from our parents and friends. More often than not, those patterns contain destructive elements. Practicing this new format will replace those negative elements with good habits that will last.

## FINAL NOTE:

Memorize these elements so you can perform them automatically:

1. Setting the tone positively
2. Letting your partner off the hook
3. Presenting and repeating back
4. Demonstrating empathy
5. Be willing to solve the problem
6. Create a resolution
7. And a guarantee if you need it

Again, if you find that you're having serious problems communicating and your partner is not willing to resolve conflicts according to this pattern for effective conflict resolution, and if you want to continue the relationship, seek a professional counselor.

*Your partner is not perfect, and neither are you!*

No one will ever be exactly like you. Although you and your partner will have many things in common, there will be issues in which you must learn to compromise in order to have a lasting and happy relationship.

To compromise is to settle differences by mutual concessions. It may sound easy and sometimes it is. When it's difficult, it's good to have the right skills to create the right compromise.

# *The Art*
## OF
# COMPROMISE

# STEP #2
## THE ART OF COMPROMISE ASSIGNMENT

Following are some guidelines to help.

**AN ISSUE COMES UP**

In a discussion with your partner you discover that you have a fundamental difference of opinion. The issue could be:

1. What kind of honeymoon do you want?
2. Where you would live if you married.
3. Activities you want to pursue and your partner doesn't.
4. If you want children or not.
5. If your partner wants to travel and you don't.
6. Differences in financial philosophies.
7. Religious Differences
8. Political Differences

**These are just a few from an endless list of possibilities.**

**WHAT SHOULD YOU DO?**

1. To begin the process of compromise, first clarify the differences. In other words, state the issue without emotion.
2. Next, ask each other, "Are you willing to compromise?"
3. If the answers are "yes," for both, you have something to work with. If "no" from either or both of you, you have a problem.

# HERE ARE TWO EXAMPLES TO PONDER:

## 1. A NEGATIVE EXAMPLE

There is a thought-provoking book and movie entitled, "Dodsworth." It's a story about Sam Dodsworth, a car manufacturing tycoon, and his wife of twenty years, Fran. Now that their only Dodsworth descendant is married, Sam decides to sell his business so that he and Fran can enjoy a second honeymoon in Europe. Once on board a transatlantic cruise to Europe, it becomes clear that Sam and Fran have different agendas. Fran wants to be romanced and live a life in high society. She wants to be admired, adored, and loved. Sam wants to learn new things and have a companion who will share his interests. He refuses to dance with his wife, and instead encourages her to dance with other men on board ship. Once in Europe Sam invites Fran to go touring with him. He is excited to see the sights and learn the history. Fran can't be bothered. She succumbs to the charms of other men. They ignore each other's needs without any compromise or attempt to renew the original love they had for each other. Rather than being on a second honeymoon together, they start living separate lives. Their actions escalate until there is no other option but divorce.

It would have taken very little to fulfill each other's desires. With a well-formed compromise, Sam could have agreed to dance, attend society events and romance his wife, and Fran could have agreed to tour with her husband and learn about the sights they visited.

If you can obtain a copy of this classic movie, watch it together and discuss. It's a good one to see how quickly things can go wrong.

## 2. A POSITIVE EXAMPLE

My husband and I were married in Switzerland and commenced a five-week honeymoon through Europe. We were in love and getting along great until one day we were in France at a Carrefour supermarket, a huge store with groceries, clothes, books, toys, pharmacy etc. Right away when we entered, I took charge telling my new husband what to do. I had previously lived in France for a year and a half and spoke French. I just felt I should be in charge. My husband, Conrad, did not like being ordered around. We started an argument and then stopped suddenly when we realized the importance of what was happening. I said, "We need to solve this problem now or we'd better get an annulment." We laughed and talked about how we could find a compromise. After a long discussion in the bakery department, we decided that in any given situation like this, where multiple options were possible, we would decide who was the boss over that situation and the other one would follow. Since I was the expert in France, I became the boss there. Since my husband had been to Greece before, he would be in charge there. It was a terrific solution that made us both happy. We still follow that original compromise. Practicing the Art of Compromise early began a marvelous marriage for us.

# <u>NOW READ AND MEMORIZE THE FOLLOWING</u>

## COMPROMISE GUIDELINES AND FORMAT:

1. **State the issue without emotion.**

2. **Decide to compromise and discuss possible solutions.**

3. **Decide on a compromise that works for both of you and makes you both happy.**

## EXAMPLE OF FORMAT FOR COMPROMISE

After you discover in a discussion that you have differences of opinions or wants, and need to find a resolution, follow this process:

## 1. STATE THE ISSUE WITHOUT EMOTION.

**PRESENTER:** "I'd like to discuss what you once said would be an ideal honeymoon, if and when we decide to get married. You said you'd like to go to Hawaii and stay in a resort hotel for five days, doing nothing except getting to know each other."

**LISTENER:** "Yes, my ideal honeymoon would be to relax and take time to get to know each other intimately and enjoy the luxury of time together without responsibilities. It's going to be hectic just getting married. Everybody says so. And, personally, I think we'll need time to decompress. Also, we'll be away from work and I want to rest."

**PRESENTER:** "Well, I have a different view. Since I've never been to Hawaii and may never get there again, I want to see everything possible. You know me! I'm a doer. I want to see the sights and take lots of photos. I want to go on some scenic hikes and create some great memories with you."

**LISTENER:** "It sounds like we're pretty far apart on this. What can we do so we could both be happy?"

## 2. DECIDE TO COMPROMISE AND DISCUSS POSSIBLE SOLUTIONS.

**PRESENTER:** "Since we have a limited amount of time on a honeymoon, the only way we can both be happy is to find some middle ground. Would you be willing to compromise?"

**LISTENER:** "Sounds like you really want to see and tour the island. And you said you wanted to hike too. That sounds like a lot, but I'm willing to compromise as long as we get some quality time to just get to know each other and relax?"

**PRESENTER:** "OK, that's great. How about this possibility: we could spend the first day just relaxing, then tour and hike for 3 days and then 1 day at the end to decompress before coming home?"

**LISTENER:** "Nice try, but I don't think that's enough time for me. What would you think about adding 2 days to our honeymoon so I could have enough quiet time: 2 days at the beginning to decompress, 3 seeing the island, and 2 at the end to rest. I know I could get the time off work. How about you?"

**PRESENTER:** "That might be possible. Actually, it sounds pretty good, but it would cost more."

## 3. DECIDE ON A COMPROMISE THAT MAKES YOU BOTH HAPPY.

**LISTENER:** "Hmm. I can solve that right now and it would be worth it to me. I've got a little money coming from my tax return, and I could use that to cover the cost. I'd be willing to set it aside for what would be a perfect honeymoon."

**PRESENTER**: "That's very kind. If you cover that extra cost, I'm all in. Thanks for being so willing to compromise."

## NEXT, TRY THE ART OF COMPROMISE FORMAT YOURSELF ON THE NEXT PAGE.

# FORMAT FOR COMPROMISE

## 1. STATE THE ISSUE WITHOUT EMOTION

**PRESENTER:** I'd like to discuss. (*State the issue in conflict without emotion.*) _____

_____
_____
_____
_____

**LISTENER:** So you think….(*Repeat what the presenter has said to make it clear.*) _____

_____
_____
_____
_____

**LISTENER:** This is what I think about that. (*State your position on the issue.*)

_____
_____
_____
_____

**PRESENTER:** Well, I have a different view. (*State your viewpoint without emotion.*)

_____
_____
_____
_____

**LISTENER:** Sounds like we're far apart. (*State the two positions.*)

_____
_____
_____
_____

## 2. DECIDE TO COMPROMISE AND DISCUSS POSSIBLE SOLUTIONS.

**PRESENTER:** I'm willing to compromise. (*Show willingness to discuss/resolve.*) _____

_____
_____
_____

**LISTENER:** I understand your position. I'm willing too. (*Describe the conflict.*)

_____
_____
_____

**PRESENTER:** How about this as a compromise? (*State a possible compromise.*) _____

_____

_____

_____

_____

**LISTENER:** That's possible. I'd like to add…. (*State your proposed compromise.*) _____

_____

_____

_____

_____

## 3. DECIDE ON A COMPROMISE THAT MAKES YOU BOTH HAPPY.

### (*Repeat next 2 steps until agreed.*)

**PRESENTER:** I'd like to change ….. (*Propose changes until satisfied.*)

_____

_____

_____

**LISTENER:** How about….? (Propose changes until satisfied.)

_____

_____

_____

**PRESENTER:** I accept the compromise. (Repeat the compromise as you understand it.)

_____

_____

_____

_____

_____

**LISTENER:** And I agree too. (*Repeat the compromise as you understand it.*) _____

_____

_____

_____

_____

## Now reverse the roles and run through the exercise again, noting your compromise skills.

## 1. STATE THE ISSUE WITHOUT EMOTION

**PRESENTER:** I'd like to discuss. (*State the issue in conflict without emotion.*): _____

_____

_____

_____

_____

**LISTENER:** So you think….(*Repeat what the presenter has said to make it clear.*) _____

_____

_____

_____

_____

**LISTENER:** This is what I think about that. (*State your position on the issue.*)

_____

_____

_____

_____

**PRESENTER:** Well, I have a different view. (*State your viewpoint without emotion.*)

_____

_____

_____

_____

**LISTENER:** Sounds like we're far apart. (*State the two positions.*)

_____

_____

_____

_____

## 2. DECIDE TO COMPROMISE AND DISCUSS POSSIBLE SOLUTIONS.

**PRESENTER:** I'm willing to compromise. (*Show willingness to discuss/resolve.*) _____

_____

_____

_____

**LISTENER:** I understand your position. I'm willing too. (*Describe the conflict.*)

_____

_____

_____

**PRESENTER:** How about this as a compromise?
(*State a possible compromise.*) _____

_____

_____

_____

_____

_____

_____

_____

**LISTENER:** That's possible. I'd like to add....
(*State your proposed compromise.*) _____

_____

_____

_____

_____

_____

## 3. DECIDE ON A COMPROMISE THAT MAKES YOU BOTH HAPPY.

*(Repeat next 2 steps until agreed.)*

**PRESENTER:** I'd like to change ..... (*Propose changes until satisfied.*)

_____

_____

_____

**LISTENER:** How about....? (Propose changes until satisfied.)

_____

_____

_____

**PRESENTER:** I accept the compromise. (Repeat the compromise as you understand it.)

_____

_____

_____

**LISTENER:** And I agree too. (*Repeat the compromise as you understand it.*) _____

_____

_____

_____

# STEP #2
## SOME OTHER ISSUES

### THE SAFETY NET FOR UNRESOLVED DIFFERENCES

While learning the skills of conflict resolution and compromise, if you find that you can't calm down from being too angry to resolve your differences and need more time to cool off, or you are rushing off to a meeting and can't take the time to resolve the disagreement, or another emergency takes precedence, agree to provide an automatic **safety net** for maintaining a secure relationship. I have listed examples. Discuss and add your own safety net ideas that will work for you.

#### Safety Net Statements

a. No matter what feelings exist, both of you should agree ahead of time to say, "I'm sorry about this disagreement."

b. Agree to say, "I know we can work this out later. Until then, please remember, I love you very much."

c. Hug each other and reassure each other that you are still in love and have confidence that you will resolve the issue.

Remember: avoid blaming, yelling, screaming, name-calling, swearing, and other harsh statements that are difficult to repair.

## A PUNISHMENT FREE ZONE

Agree to the have and maintain the following powerful element in your relationship: "A Punishment Free Zone." This means that if your partner comes to you and tells you something bad that he/she did, right away, confessing in all honesty, and expressing deep regret, asking for forgiveness, you agree to automatically be kind and loving and forgiving. For example, "I am so sorry that I forgot to call you when I promised. I totally meant to. Then I got distracted when my brother called me. I should have told him that I'd call him back after I talked to you. Now here it is two hours later. Forgive me?" The answer in a "punishment free zone" should always be "yes, let's talk."

A punishment free zone fosters honesty and open communication. If you listen and then get angry and refuse to understand, your partner will start withholding information and even more importantly, the truth.

**Practice a Punishment Free zone.**

NOTE: This does not mean that you should become a victim from behavior that is clearly destructive to a relationship including serial cheating, abuse of any kind, breaking the law, repeated manipulation and lying, etc. Use common sense and understand that there are limits and boundaries to avoid becoming a victim.

# STEP #2 - QUESTIONNAIRE #4

## Fill out at home after the activity, and then compare the next time you meet in a punishment free zone.

1. Since you've learned the conflict resolution skills, have you had a disagreement with your partner? How was it solved? Were you satisfied with the solution?

2. Are you avoiding talk about any issue at this time? If so, why? Will your partner use the guidelines you studied together so you can solve this issue?

3. After learning these skills, are you able now to tell your partner what you think at any given time?

4. While you were practicing the conflict resolution skills, did your partner ever stop talking to you and walk away during the process? Did he/she become defensive or prideful when you discussed problems?

5. During this process of Step #2, did your partner ever ridicule you? Did your partner emotionally abuse you in any of these ways: called you "stupid" or other derogatory names, or demeaned your abilities with disdain such as "I can't believe you said that."?

6. Is your partner the type who always has to be right? Did he/she always need to have the last word during your practice sessions?

7.  How did you differ in the ways you expressed yourselves to each other?

8.  Did either one of you get angry during the practice sessions? What did you do about it?

9.  During the activity was your partner eager to learn the communication skills or did he/she think it wasn't important or valuable?

10. During the activity and questionnaires did you get into an argument? Did you solve it using the conflict management skills?

**REMEMBER:** Abusive language, angry outbursts, and refusal to improve and learn positive conflict resolution skills, are red flags and must be resolved.

# STEP # 2

## CONCEPTS TO CONSIDER

By learning these important conflict resolution skills, you are discovering the keys to solving your problems. You are on the road to a wonderful relationship with a partner who is willing to communicate with you to resolve issues. However, if your partner is not willing to resolve conflicts with you, or he/she balks at your attempts to learn how to solve your problems by improving communication skills, reevaluate your relationship. See a professional counselor. Obtain help before you go any further.

*Jackie had come from an emotionally abusive home. Her father exercised excessive controlling behavior and always had to be right. Jackie learned to keep her emotions to herself. She would never tell her father her true feelings about anything. When she met and fell in love with Taj, an outgoing, fun loving guy, she began to open up. When they had their first fight she immediately withdrew and refused to discuss the problem. Taj loved Jackie and understood the problems they had in communicating with each other. He didn't want to have problems after their engagement and immediately sought out a professional counselor. After three months of learning how to resolve conflicts together, they became engaged and later married. Ten years later they are still happily married and enjoying a healthy relationship.*

Learn,
Practice &
Resolve

**R**EMEMBER: There is great satisfaction in a relationship with a partner who enjoys resolving conflicts through positive conflict resolution skills.

**AFTER:** Now that you've completed Step #2, alone at home, record in your journal your reactions. After a thorough review, determine if you're ready to take the next step.

The past, especially, plays a significant part in any relationship and it's important that two people, who decide to share their lives intimately, know as much as possible about each other.

# STEP #3

## WHERE HAVE YOU BEEN
## AND WHERE ARE YOU GOING?

## INTRODUCTION

By the time you're ready for a serious relationship and possible marriage, you have had many experiences that affect who you have become. Some of you have been married previously. Others have had trouble with relationships or have very little experience. Many have graduated from college or have advanced degrees, while others may not have graduated from high school. You might have been in the military. You might have traveled extensively or never left your hometown. Some of you have many siblings, some fewer, and some of you have lived life as an only child. You may have grown up poor, or maybe rich. You may have started a business or worked for someone else. Whatever you have done, you have a complex set of experiences which have helped to form you.

Some experiences are negative and have had profound effects on your psyche. Maybe you had to kill people when you were in the military. Maybe you were abused as a little child or maybe even as a young adult. Whatever has happened, you cannot change it. It simply is.

The most important question now is where will you go next? Step #3 is designed to help you deal with the past, present and future in your relationship. The past, especially, plays a significant part in any relationship and it's important that two people, who decide to share their lives intimately, know as much as possible about each other.

This step takes you on a journey to discover where you and your partner have been, are now, and where you are going. Enjoy the process.

# STEP # 3

## INSTRUCTIONS

*Family Issues, Cultural backgrounds, Religious backgrounds, Romance, Your Love Languages and Sex*

1. **Preparation:**
   a. Pick a weekend that you can spend most of the time together.
   b. Separately, read the entire step 3.
   c. Separately, fill out questionnaires #1 through #7 except for the parts you fill out together.

2. **Plan:**
   a. Plan the next three activities in any order that works for both of you.

3. **Activity 1: Select a day to visit each other's parents and/or extended family.**
   a. Make it a breakfast, lunch or some other activity where you can get to know each other and each other's family. Preferably on a Saturday or Sunday. If they are too far away, use Skype or Facetime so you can see each other.
   b. Discuss with other family members their lives, especially their marriages if appropriate.

4. **Activity 2: Go on what you would consider to be a romantic date.**
   a. Pick a restaurant that's not too crowded or noisy so you can talk freely.
   b. Avoid a movie, play or any other date where you don't talk.
   c. To make it romantic, dress up. For some people it might be fun to go to a thrift shop together and as part of the activity, buy a beautiful vintage dress and/or a vintage suit and tie.
   d. Prepare a list of romantic tunes on your smart phone for the drive.
   e. Bring your filled-out questionnaires and, over dinner, discuss your answers.
   f. After dinner, go somewhere to dance where's it's not too loud so you can talk. (even on a rooftop with a boombox)

5. **Activity 3: Visit each other's church or a place you consider spiritual.**
   a. If both of you are religious, attend each other's church and talk about the beliefs and how important church is to each other.
   b. If only one is religious, attend that church and find a place to discuss spiritual thoughts with each other. If both are non-religious, spend time discussing spiritual thoughts wherever you might find inspiration.

6. **AFTER:**
   a. Record in your journal your feelings about the issues discussed in this step.
   b. And most importantly, decide if you want to take the next step with your partner.

# STEP #3 - QUESTIONNAIRE #1
## FAMILY BACKGROUND

1.  Describe your relationship with your Father.

2.  Describe your relationship with your Mother.

3.  What are the strengths of your Father?

4.  What are the strengths of your Mother?

5.  What are the weaknesses of your Father?

6.  What are the weaknesses of your Mother?

7.  Are you more like your Mother or Father?

8.  What are strengths you feel you have inherited from your Father?

9.  What are weaknesses you feel you have inherited from your Father?

10. What are strengths you feel you have inherited from your Mother?

11. What are weaknesses you feel you have inherited from your Mother?

12. How do you not want to be like your Father?

13. How do you not want to be like your Mother?

14. Do you have unresolved resentments towards your Mother or Father? Describe.

**STEP #3 – QUESTIONNAIRE #1 (Continued)**

15. If you have resentments, how can you resolve them?

16. How can you avoid taking these resentments into your marriage?

17. What qualities in your parent's marriage do you want to duplicate in your own?

18. What qualities in your parents' marriage do you want to avoid?

19. List challenges that your parents had to face such as financial loss, being out of work, medical issues, and death of a loved one, and any other crises. Describe how they responded to them emotionally and/or intellectually. How did they resolve them?

20. How did your parents' problems affect your life? How did you deal with these issues? Have you resolved them now?

21. List problems you encountered in your family such as abuse, neglect, rivalry, accidents, moving to a new high school, etc. Have you resolved these issues and problems? If so, how? If not, what will you do to resolve them now?

22. Do you agree or disagree with the methods your parents used to solve their problems? Why?

23. How do you usually solve conflicts and problems in your life? Is it the same as your parents or different? Describe.

24. Do your parents approve of your partner? If no, describe why.

25. Are any of your parents' objections valid? Why? Look at them with an open mind.

26. Should you seriously pay attention to your parents' concerns? Should you continue courting to investigate their objections?

27. What will be the influence of your future in-laws in your marriage? If they have influence, what will be the hierarchy of their authority if you marry?

28. If your in-laws attempt to interfere in your marriage, and you don't want their help, how will you handle the situation?

**STEP # 3– QUESTIONNAIRE # 1 Continued**

29. If your parents insult your spouse and he/she never wants to speak to them again, how would you handle this situation?

30. How much will your future be integrated into your in-laws' lives? How many times a year will you see them? How many visits will be expected? What are your partner's desires on this subject? Do you agree?

31. Do you like your prospective in-laws?

32. What do you like about them?

33. What do you dislike about your prospective in-laws?

34. What do you see as areas of future conflict with in-laws?

35. What rules and boundaries should you have regarding future in-laws? Write them down.

# STEP # 3– QUESTIONNAIRE #2

## WHEN YOU GET TOGETHER, DISCUSS THE FOLLOWING QUESTIONS:

1. Comparing your responses to the questions above with your partner, do you agree or disagree on the kind of marriage relationship with family and in-laws you want to have? Discuss.

2. How will you and your partner resolve problems regarding family and in-laws that may arise in a future marriage? Discuss.

3. If there are parental objections about your relationships on either or both sides, how are you going to deal with the disapproval? How will you protect each other from negative comments/behavior from family and in-laws? Discuss.

4. If you have serious disagreements in this area of family and in-laws, write them down here. If you both agree to find a compromise, use the process in Step #2 to work through your disagreement to find a solution you can both agree on.

# STEP #3 – QUESTIONNAIRES #1 & #2
## CONCEPTS TO CONSIDER

Our families in our early life have a profound effect on us. It's important to understand that influence, and how it might differ for our partner. Problems in marriage often have a root in something a person learned or experienced in their original family. Sometimes, it's difficult to discern because our experience can be different from our partner's and we may not be equipped to understand.

Tony Robbins, author and life coach, used to tell a story about his marriage. He described that he grew up in a family that would confront conflict directly and work it out in the room until it was solved. Not facing it by leaving the room was the worst thing you could do. His wife grew up in a family that avoided conflict by walking out of a room. She believed that was the way to solve disagreements. Robbins called these two opposite behaviors "scripts" because they indicated automatic "scripted" behavior learned in their original homes. This difference in how to handle conflict caused trouble in his marriage. Without realizing that they had different scripts that they followed automatically, the disagreement could not be resolved, and would escalate to where it was unbearable. Fortunately, through discussion with his wife later on, he discovered the "scripts" and was able to set a new pattern in his marriage.

If your parents, relatives and/or friends disapprove of your partner, seriously weigh the objections before you move forward with your relationship. Are their objections something you should consider? Ask yourself: "Are you convinced, without a doubt, that your relationship will last in spite of their objections?" Make sure your love is strong enough to endure opposition. It's important for you to be ready to support and stand up for your partner and be unified in front of family. Your partner is the most important person in your life. You must defend and protect him/her against outside negativity. If you can't do this, seek professional counseling.

*Erin and Tom married straight out of college. They were both twenty-two years old and each other's first love. They had an elaborate society wedding at an exclusive club. Tom's parents gave the newlyweds a small brick Tudor house for a wedding present. Erin's parents, living on modest schoolteacher salaries, gave the young couple a set of china purchased at a discount store.*

*After the wedding, trouble in paradise began. First Tom went to work for his mother, Martha, in the family business. Martha insisted that the young couple spend monthly dinners at her home. This was an innocuous sounding request. However, Martha did not like Erin. Erin wanted to love Martha but her constant barbs at dinnertime offended her. Martha had verbally expressed her dislike of Erin before the wedding, but Tom turned a deaf ear. Now the objections were expressed to Erin directly. Martha didn't like the way Erin dressed. Her clothes looked low class. Martha asked her to change her hairstyle. Martha didn't like Erin's job and wanted her to work in the family business.*

*At home Erin would plead with Tom to defend her at the family dinners. He would reply, "I can't. I have to keep the peace because I work with her and I'm going to inherit the business someday. I don't want to get on her bad side."*

*Erin with contempt would say, "Who do you love, her or me?"*

*"Erin that's not fair. You know I love you." He would state firmly.*

*"No, you love your Mother more than you love me, or you'd defend me."*

*And so the arguments would escalate, each time worse than the last. Finally, Erin went to a counselor and realized that she didn't have to stay in a marriage that brought her unhappiness. After only two years of marriage, they divorced. We could say it was thanks to in-law objections, interference, and Tom's lack of loyalty to his new wife.*

Understanding habits gained from our original families, and successfully dealing with negative opinions are critical to creating a great relationship.

REMEMBER: **When you marry, you also marry his/her family!** The unresolved differences you uncover in this pre-engagement counseling course are warning signs to you. Be open-minded. Either resolve the issues or seriously consider dissolving your relationship.

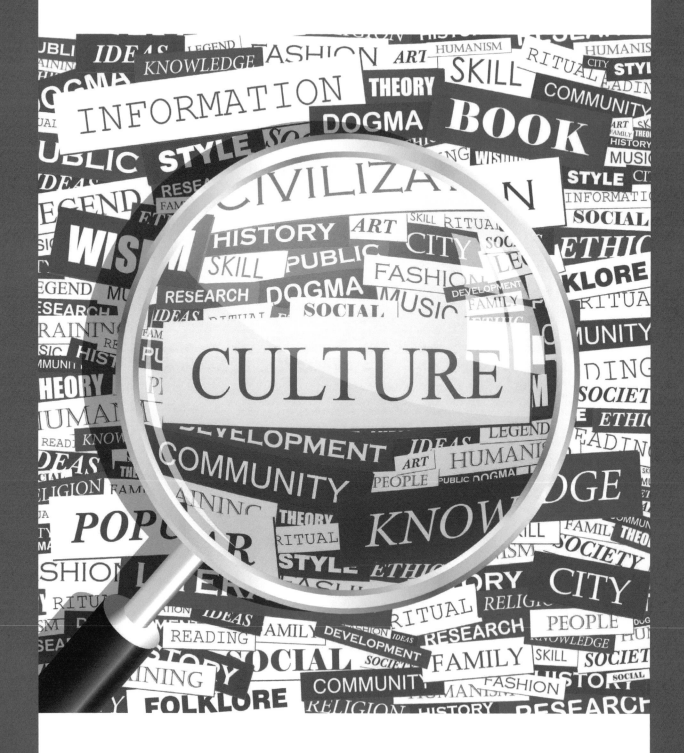

# STEP #3 – QUESTIONNAIRE #3

## CULTURAL BACKGROUND

1. Describe the role of the father and mother from your cultural background. This may be a religious culture you come from such as Jewish, Christian, Buddhist, Muslim, or a country's culture such as Iran, Africa, or South America where daily life may be very different from the country you both currently live in.

2. Do you want your future husband/wife to fulfill the same cultural role described in question number one? What are your expectations?

**When you get together, discuss your answers about cultural backgrounds. Then answer and discuss the following questions together.**

1. Do you foresee any issues or problems with cultural differences? What are they?

2. Are you completely aware of each other's cultural background? If not, what do you need to do to more fully understand each other in this area?

3. Are there any lifestyles that will be brought into your home together that you cannot accept? What are they? Will these present a source of conflict in a future marriage?

4. Do your backgrounds conflict regarding any basic philosophies? How?

5. If you have discovered potential conflicts, how can you compromise?

# STEP #3 – QUESTIONNAIRE #3
## CONCEPTS TO CONSIDER

If your partner cannot accept your culture and refuses to accept the roles dictated by it, are you prepared to abandon your culture to live as he/she wants? Weigh the pros and cons.

If you are still worried and think that you should just go along with your partner's desires for now, and then insist on him/her following your cultural roles and lifestyle after the marriage, think again! This choice will inevitably end in unhappiness and potential divorce.

*Janelle was ecstatic the day Aman proposed marriage on top of the Seattle Space Needle. He was tan, muscular, and oozed with charm. She was tall, willowy, and delicate. They met by happenstance. Janelle, eager to furnish her first apartment in style, wandered into a small Persian carpet store in Pioneer Square advertising 50% off. Aman waited on her. It was love at first sight as they gazed into each other's eyes. Buying the carpet became secondary after Aman asked her to dinner that night. Aman was romantic and swept her off her feet. She was head over heels in love. It was a whirlwind courtship and now they were engaged. It had never dawned on Janelle that they came from two separate worlds.*

*He seemed like any other all-American boy until Aman drove Janelle home to Los Angeles to meet his mother and father. Aman's mother was the epitome of the professional homemaker. While the men entertained Janelle, Aman's mother spent hours working in the kitchen preparing exotic Middle Eastern dishes. That weekend Janelle asked Aman for the first time, "Do you want me to be like your mother? I mean cook three meals a day for you, clean, iron, and mend your clothes?" Aman was stunned by the question.*

*"Why, yes. You don't have to work after we're married. I'll take care of you," he offered lovingly.*

*"But I want to work," Janelle insisted. "I'm a career girl, not a homemaker."*

*After all the romance, it was difficult to face reality. They were talking about each other's expectations of cultural roles in a marriage. And they were very different. Very different! At the end of the weekend they separated with heated words.*

*Later, Aman called Janelle on the phone. "Janelle, I love you. Let's not let something so unimportant come between us. Let's put our differences aside until after we're married. Our love is stronger than whether or not you stay home."*

*"You're right. Love can conquer all." She acquiesced. The wedding plans continued until they were married in a lovely garden ceremony in her parent's backyard overlooking Mt. Rainier.*

*What happened after the wedding? Did it end happily ever after? I wish I could report that it did. Unfortunately, Janelle and Aman failed to do their homework. Because they didn't work out a plan before the wedding, heated arguments occurred again. When Aman asked Janelle to quit her job and stay at home, she refused. Three months later, stressed out by her new husband's incessant harassing, she resigned from work and assumed the role of full-time homemaker and lover. Now at home all the time, Janelle wanted to join an exercise club. Aman wouldn't allow it. He thought that it wasn't proper now that she was married. He wouldn't let her volunteer for charity organizations, and he refused to allow her the opportunity to join a book club with friends. He insisted on homemade cooking every day. She learned to please him with all his favorite foods, but after the first and then second baby was born, Aman became more controlling than ever.*

*In Aman's culture, the man worked in the world and the woman stayed at home. He was the decision-maker and the Patriarch of the family. All who lived under his roof obeyed him. Janelle came from a culture in which her mother was part of every major decision in the household. Her mother and father were a team. Aman opened his own carpet store without consulting Janelle. Later he sold it at a great loss. Then he jumped right back in again, opening a dry cleaning store, a business about which he knew almost nothing. Janelle was horrified by how he made decisions. When her checks were refused at the grocery store, she agonized thinking that they must be on the verge of bankruptcy. Janelle begged Aman to let her go back to work, or at least help out at the new business. Aman refused.*

*Janelle wanted and needed the stimulation of working outside the home. Since Aman wouldn't let her, she decided that she could earn money to help out by working at home. Janelle thought it would be relatively easy to find computer work that could be outsourced from her home. Surely her husband would agree. She wouldn't have to leave her two little toddlers. It would be the best of both worlds. Aman refused to give his permission. The thought of her working at all was an insult to his manhood and ability as the breadwinner of the family. Four years later the marriage ended in an ugly divorce with custody battles over their two children.*

If only Janelle and Aman had faced the cultural differences between them prior to marriage. Aman needed a partner that bought into his culture completely, and Janelle needed a husband who allowed her to have a life outside the role of homemaker.

Another case ended quite differently. *Chang came from a traditional Chinese background and was steeped in his family roots. Amy, a New Yorker with Italian ancestry, was excited about the prospects of marrying Chang. They began to plan the wedding and she purchased her wedding dress. However, as they got to know each other better, they sensed something was wrong. They asked to try my yet untested "Premarital Counseling Course." As they proceeded through the course, Chang realized that Amy was not for him. He could see that what he really wanted was a clone of his mother. He needed someone from a traditional Chinese background who would be: quiet, self-effacing, always working in the home serving his family, and putting other's needs above her own. Amy was beautiful and Chang loved her, but love was not enough. She was a free spirited, gregarious woman who lived for her career and nights out with her friends. He knew that the cultural gulf between them was an impediment to a harmonious engagement and future marriage. Although it was difficult to part, they made the right decision.*

I have known other marriages where two people from very different background cultures worked together just fine. In some cases, however, one or both were not interested in taking their culture into the marriage. In other cases, some compromises had to be made to make the marriage work. You must be diligent to know the truth.

## Know your partner's culture and how it affects him/her.

# RELIGION & SPIRITUALITY

"A person who marries with the intent of changing his/her spouse later is doomed to disappointment and potential divorce."

# STEP #3 – QUESTIONNAIRE #4
## RELIGIOUS BACKGROUND

*"A person who marries with the intent of changing his/her spouse later is doomed to disappointment and potential divorce."*

1. Are you of the same religion?

2. If you are of the same religion, do you share the same zeal?

3. If the answer is no, do you foresee problems? What are they?

4. If your religions are different, which church do you plan to attend?

5. In which church will you raise your children?

6. Have you had disagreements over religion? Were the issues in conflict resolved?

7. Do your parents disapprove of your partner's religion?

8. Do you secretly think that you will convert your partner to your religion after the wedding?

9. Have you prayed to know if your partner is the right one for you? If so, what were your spiritual feelings after you prayed?

10. How do you feel about voluntary church service? Is it important to you? How about your partner?

11. Can you support your partner if he/she is very active in his/her church and gives many hours of service?

12. How do you feel about paying tithes or offerings to the church you attend? How about your partner?

# STEP #3 – QUESTIONNAIRE #4

## CONCEPTS TO CONSIDER

During your discussion, have you found your partner to be more spiritually inclined than you? How do you feel about that? On the other hand, are you extremely religious and your partner irreligious? If yes, talk about the reality of one going to church and the other one playing golf, working in the garden, or hiking on the weekends without you. Will this eventually cause problems? Can you compromise now? Could you take turns going to church and playing golf? Is a compromise possible? If not, consider this a serious area of concern.

**Do not repeat this old story:** *Karen was a devout Catholic. She would never even entertain the idea of missing Mass. At one time she had considered becoming a Nun. Her parents were upset when she decided to marry Dustin, a non-Catholic and self-professed agnostic. Karen insisted. They loved each other and she felt certain that after the wedding he would eventually embrace her faith. Already he had spent two Sundays attending Mass with her. She thought that this was a sign of a future baptism. They never talked about it. She merely assumed it. Her plan was flawed because it was one-sided. After the wedding, he made it clear that he had no intention of joining her church. She was shocked. He told her that he couldn't believe that his attendance at two Masses misled her into thinking that he was interested in her religion. He thought that he had made it perfectly clear that he was a non-believer.*

*Now married, he didn't feel he had to go to church with her out of courtesy. Besides, golf was far more important to him. As the years proceeded, Dustin met a lovely single girl at the country club golf course and began playing rounds of golf with her each Sunday. At first it was in a group of others and then they began finding excuses to play together alone. Karen knew how to play golf too but was unavailable to play on Sundays. Another woman filled her spot. A long-term affair ensued. Divorce followed.*

**The following scenario works:** *Edmond and Larissa met on a blind date. Larissa talked about her church frequently during the course of the evening. She talked about her experiences being a missionary in a foreign country. At the end of the date, Edmond expressed his feelings.*

*"I can see that your religion means more to you than anything else in the world. So, before we date formally, I better first get to know about your church. If I like it and want it in my life, then we could date seriously. What do you think?"*

*Larissa was impressed, "Wow! I can't believe how insightful you are. You're right about my religion. It does matter to me deeply. I like your plan. It's the right way to go. Then neither of us will get hurt nor have false expectations."*

*Larissa taught Edmond all about her church and he attended the Sunday meetings regularly for the next three months. During this time he fell in love with its principles, practices, philosophies, and way of life. He joined her church and then their courtship began. Twenty-seven years later they are still happily married.* **Religious unity is important in a marriage.**

**"A husband and wife who attend church together grow together and stay together!"**

# ROMANCE

"Romance is kept alive because of conscious effort on a daily basis."

# STEP #3 – QUESTIONNAIRE #5
## ROMANTIC BACKGROUND

1. Is your partner romantic? Describe.

2. Does your partner give you the daily kind of love that you need? Describe.

3. What kind of romance do you expect in a relationship and a marriage?

4. Does your partner bring you unexpected gifts, cards and flowers? Is it important to you that this continues after a marriage?

5. Does your partner acknowledge and celebrate your birthday and holidays with you?

6. How important are regular/weekly dates with your partner? Would you expect the same after marriage?

7. What do you consider a romantic date? Does your partner agree?

8. Is your partner interested in what you have to say? Does he/she prefer to read, watch TV, or play on the computer, or be alone rather than talk to you?

9. Do you think your partner has unrealistic expectations about romance? Explain.

**STEP #3 – QUESTIONNAIRE #5 - Continued**

10. Do you feel that your expectations about romance are reasonable? Are you concerned that your partner might not have the desire or inclination to satisfy your needs?

11. What can you do to ensure the level of romance you expect in your future relationship?

12. Make a list of the things your partner has done that made you feel the most loved.

1) _____

2) _____

3) _____

4) _____

5) _____

6) _____

7) _____

8) _____

9) _____

10) _____

# STEP #3 - QUESTIONNAIRE #6
## DISCOVERING YOUR LOVE LANGUAGE

Everyone has criteria for how they feel loved or their "Love Language." We define five different ones here. **WHAT IS YOUR LOVE LANGUAGE?** Answer the following questions to determine yours.

Circle the letter of the one you need and want the most! You may have multiple ones that apply. Just circle the most important one.

1. Which of the following do you like most?
   a. I like to be told every day that my partner loves me.
   b. I like to spend time with my partner talking and/or doing activities together: sports or other mutually enjoyed activities.
   c. I like surprise gifts such as flowers, candy, jewelry, or other little gifts often.
   d. I like my partner to do things for me like paint my bedroom, fix my car, etc.
   e. I like to cuddle on the couch with my partner.

2. Which one of the following makes you the happiest?
   a. When my partner tells me that I'm handsome or/beautiful.
   b. When my partner asks me to go with him/her while he/she is doing errands or other activities so we can talk and just enjoy being together.
   c. When my partner takes me shopping and buys me a gift.
   d. When my partner gets my car washed or does an errand/task for me.
   e. When my partner hugs me at a party or touches me as he/she passes by.

3. Which one do you need on a regular basis the most?
   a. When my partner compliments me on something I've done?
   b. When my partner wants to spend time with me even if we are doing different activities in the same room.
   c. When my partner brings me things I've been wanting.
   d. When my partner does a chore for me without me asking for it to be done.
   e. When he/she gives me daily non-sexual touches like an embrace, a pat on the back, and unexpected tender caresses.

4. Which one makes you feel loved the most?
   a. When he/she notices me and tells others about things he/she appreciates about me.
   b. When he/she takes time out of his/her busy day to be with me.
   c. When he/she gives me a gift for no reason, just because.
   d. When he/she knows I'm so busy that I can't get something done and he/she does it for me.
   e. When he/ she gives me public displays of affection.

Add up your a's, b's, c's, d's, & e's.

a's_____   b's_____   c's_____   d's_____   e's_____

*Check out the Love Language definitions on the next page.*

*Love Languages\** are defined by what a person needs most to feel loved. Below are five categories. You may have one as dominant or a multiple.

**If you selected mainly a's in your answers, your Love Language is:**

## WORDS OF AFFIRMATION.

This means that you need to hear that you are loved regularly. You need to have at least five compliments or words of acknowledgement a day. For example: "you are handsome/beautiful; you did a great job cleaning the car; you are the best partner ever; you are so thoughtful; how did I get so lucky to attract you into my life; you mean the world to me; I can't live without you; that dress looks so sexy on you; you look great in that suit, etc."

**If you selected mainly b's your Love Language is:**

## QUALITY TIME

Some people just need to be with each other, or near each other. It doesn't even matter what they are doing. Have you ever noticed that little children need to play in the kitchen near their mother or father? They just need the security of them being nearby. Some people need lots of time spent together. Some people fulfill this by exercising together, traveling together, reading together, or playing sports together, etc.

**If you selected mainly c's, your Love Language is:**

## GIFTS AND SURPRISES

This means that you need to receive surprise gifts of love from your partner often. Flowers, cards, candy, and gifts that say, "I was thinking about you and thought you'd like this." This person equates love with gifts.

**If you selected mainly d's, your Love Language is:**

## ACTS OF SERVICE

This means that you feel loved the most when your partner does things for you such as: hanging pictures on the wall, fixing the leaking faucet, painting a room in your house/apartment, cooking your favorite meal, washing your car, sewing a button on your shirt or coat, driving your lunch to you because you forgot it at home, etc.

**If you selected mainly e's your Love Language is:**

## NON- SEXUAL PHYSICAL TOUCHES

This means that you need cuddling or touch on a daily basis. Perhaps just a touch on the shoulder as your partner passes by makes you feel loved. Daily hugs, kisses on the cheek, physical connection with someone you love tells you that you are loved.

*\*Based on the book: The 5 Love Languages by Gary D. Chapman, PhD.*

# STEP #3 – QUESTIONNAIRE #6

## CONCEPTS TO CONSIDER

I will never forget a couple that called me up at 10:00pm on a Tuesday night. They were in crisis. I asked my husband if he would mind if I invited Sharon and Will over for a spiritual counseling session. He nodded his approval.

*Sharon was so upset with Will that she wanted a divorce. She had asked Will to fix her leaky kitchen faucet two years ago. He never responded. As I questioned, I uncovered other chores that Will had not done. He hadn't mowed the lawn in the spring or the summer. When Sharon would ask him to do these tasks, he would say, "I will in a minute," or "I'll get to that on Saturday." Saturday would come and go with no results.*

*Sharon was tired of doing her own chores and her husband's as well. She said: "If he loved me, he'd do the chores." As we talked, I noticed that he was sniffling. I asked if he needed a tissue. He said it was his allergies.*

*"Allergies?" I asked. "Tell me about your allergies," I queried. It turned out that Will was allergic to grass and most other plant life, especially in the Spring and Summer.*

*I said, "No wonder you didn't mow the lawn. Why didn't you tell your wife?"*

*After extensive questioning, and evasive answers, he finally broke down and said, "I was embarrassed. I was afraid she wouldn't marry me. As a boy, kids made fun me. They called me names: wuss, pansy, girlie, and others. I didn't want to appear unmanly to my wife. Besides, my parents always told me that my allergies were psychological. I thought they might go away after we got married. The more I tried to hide it, the more Sharon got mad and just did the chores herself."*

*"Oh Will," Sharon expressed with a note of tenderness in her voice. "Why didn't you tell me? I want you to go to a doctor right away. They have medicine for allergies."*

*I interrupted. "Excuse me if I sound rude, what do allergies have to do with fixing a leaky faucet?"*

*Will looked sheepishly at me. "About the leaky faucets, I simply don't know how to fix them, and I didn't want to admit it. I just wanted to be a man, a real man in the eyes of my wife." I told him that the result he created was the exact opposite of what he wanted. A real man does his chores or hires someone to do them.*

*Sharon was getting upset. She said: "Was I so terrible that you wouldn't tell me these things?" Will answered: "Well, I guess it goes back to the fact that I had to compete with other men to win Sharon's hand, and I didn't ever want anything to make her think I was anything less. I'm so sorry Sharon."*

*After another hour of working through the problems and planning solutions, and teaching Will that doing the chores was Sharon's love language, they left my house that night happier than they had been since their honeymoon. Will got medical help for his allergies and now mows the lawn with quiet satisfaction. They reworked their budget to accommodate a plumber when needed.*

**J**UST THINK. If he knew the importance of her love language, he might have taken care of the problem earlier—*instead of two years of unhappiness in their marriage.*

# STEP #3– QUESTIONNAIRE #7
## PAST RELATIONSHIPS

1. Are there any past relationships in your life that are still unresolved? Describe in detail.

2. Are you still in love (in any way) with any previous partner or if you are divorced, a past spouse? Describe your feelings.

3. Is this relationship a rebound from another? What didn't work then, and how have you resolved the issue with your new partner?

4. Have you told your partner about past relationships? Will the past have any negative effect on your relationship with him/her?

5. If you are divorced with children, how would you like your partner to parent your children: Full authority, No authority, or something in-between?

6. If your partner is divorced with children, how would you like to handle your role as a new step-parent: Full authority, No authority, or something in-between?

7. If your partner has had past sexual experiences or problems, will it get in the way of your future relationship?

8.  How do you feel about sexual behavior other than intercourse? Do you think it is wrong/right?

9.  What kinds of sexual behavior between partners do you think would be wrong and make you uncomfortable?

10. What are your sexual expectations when you are on a honeymoon?

11. What are your sexual expectations in a marriage?

12. Should you have rules in your marriage regarding sexual activity? What would they be?

13. Do you feel that it is wrong to deny a partner sex for any reason? What about frequency: more than one week? Two weeks? A month?

14. What should be done if one is feeling driven to have sex and the other is too tired?

15. Should you have rules about sex during an illness of a partner? What would they be?

16. How do you feel about sex during a pregnancy?

17. How will you handle sexual disappointments or differences if they happen in your relationship?

18. Does your partner have trouble talking about sex? If so, what can you do so you can both have an open and honest discussion about the subject?

19. Is there anything you fear or worry about in your future sexual relationship? For example, are you worried about the acceptance of any part of your body by your partner?

20. What do you think about joking or kidding in your sexual relationship?

21. If your partner feels inadequate about any part of his/her body, and if you had the money, would you approve of plastic surgery?

**STEP #3– QUESTIONNAIRE #7 – Continued**

22. How do you feel about masturbation? Is there any time in a relationship that you feel it would be appropriate?

23. Have you ever had a homosexual or lesbian sexual experience? If so, do you still feel same sex attraction?

24. Are you in any way confused about your sexuality? Is gender an issue with you besides what you are physically? If so, will this affect your relationship negatively?

# STEP # 3 – QUESTIONNAIRE #7

## CONCEPTS TO CONSIDER

Romance is important in healthy relationships. Keeping it alive requires constant attention. Patterns are set during dating. If your partner doesn't talk much to you now, he/she will probably do less after you are married. Talk time is essential in marriage because it is during that time that problems are resolved, and your relationship is deepened. During courtship, start a pattern of healthy conversation. That means that you will have to plan dates that allow talking. Movies and watching television are the worst dates for this purpose, unless you plan discussions after viewing.

Another critical area that ensures romance is quality dating. If you are just "hanging out" with your partner, you are missing opportunities to get to know each other better through meaningful experiences. If you develop habits during courtship of interesting dates, you will most likely follow the same pattern after marriage.

If your partner does not understand your love language or vice versa, this can cause problems. You and your partner deserve to be loved in the ways you both want.

If you are still in love with another person or have unresolved romantic attachments to him/her, make sure you don't move ahead in your new relationship without dealing with this critical issue. It's not fair to your partner and your future together if you don't. Discuss what you both might do if some past love shows up in your life again. Because the Internet makes it so much easier to find people from the past, unplanned reunions have become a common relationship breaker. A strategy thought out ahead is a good idea.

*Allen thought that it was over with his ex-girlfriend, Allison. She had dumped him for another guy. Now he was about to marry Phyllis. They never talked about his or her previous relationships. Two years after the wedding, Allison reappeared in Allen's life. She told him that she had made a terrible mistake, and that he was the only man that she had ever loved and ever would love. Allen was blown away. All of his old feelings came to the surface. They hugged and kissed and promised to get together. Allen returned home and broke the news to Phyllis. She was shocked. Why hadn't they talked about his love for his old girlfriend? She never would have married him if she had known. Now it was too late and a divorce was inevitable.*

REMEMBER: If you are struggling with any sexual issues, it is imperative that you stop the engagement plans and seek professional counseling. This area is especially difficult if you are currently having sexual relations with your partner. I recommend that all sexual activity (except kissing and hugging) be avoided until marriage. With clear minds and emotions, you will better be able to discuss this critical area. Abstinence improves your pre-engagement and pre-marital relationship, so you can truly see what is important. One of the most common causes of divorce is sex. Understanding how each of you feels about this important aspect of marriage is critical. If you have serious physical or psychological issues about sex, it's best to get professional advice.

***Since we are talking about sharing confidential information, this is a good time to consider signing a Non-Disclosure Agreement between the two of you. It's located on the next page. Please sign the agreement in each other's book if you so desire.***

# Non-Disclosure and Confidentiality Agreement

This Non-Disclosure and Confidentiality Agreement is entered into as of the _____ day of _____, _____ (the "Effective Date") by and between _____ and _____ who have indicated an interest in exploring a potential relationship. In connection with the respective evaluation of the relationship, each party, may provide or gain access to confidential information. The party disclosing its Confidential Information to the other party is hereafter referred to as the "Disclosing Party." The party receiving the Confidential Information of the Disclosing Party is hereafter referred to as the "Receiving Party." In consideration for being furnished Confidential Information, _____ and _____ agree as follows:

1. **Confidential Information.** The term "Confidential Information" as used in this Agreement shall mean any data or information that is sensitive material and not generally known to the public, including financial information and confidential history.

2. **Obligation to Maintain Confidentiality.** With respect to Confidential Information:
   a. The Receiving Party agrees to retain the Confidential Information of the Disclosing Party in strict confidence, to protect the security, integrity and confidentiality of such information and to not permit unauthorized access to or unauthorized use, disclosure, publication or dissemination of Confidential Information except in conformity with this Agreement;
   b. Upon the termination of this Agreement, the Receiving Party will ensure that all documents, memoranda, notes and other writings or electronic records prepared by it that include or reflect any Confidential Information are returned or destroyed as directed by the Disclosing Party;
   d. If there is an unauthorized disclosure or loss of any of the Confidential Information by the Receiving Party, it will promptly, at its own expense, notify the Disclosing Party in writing and take all actions as may be necessary or reasonably requested by the Disclosing Party to minimize any damage to the Disclosing Party as a result of the disclosure or loss; and
   e. The obligation not to disclose Confidential Information shall survive the termination of this Agreement, and at no time will the Receiving Party be permitted to disclose Confidential Information,

3. **Termination.** This Agreement will terminate on the earlier of: (a) the written agreement of the parties to terminate this Agreement; (b) the consummation of the relationship; or (c) the termination of the relationship.

IN WITNESS WHEREOF, the parties hereto have executed this Agreement as of the date first written above.

By: _____          _____
     printed name                                       signature

By: _____          _____
     printed name                                       signature

Laura Nielson Denke

# What about HEALTH:

## Physical

## Mental

# FINANCIAL and ...
# INTEGRITY?

# STEP #4

## INTRODUCTION

Now that you've reached Step #4, it's time to take on the BIG deal-breakers in any relationship: Health, Money and Integrity. Everything in Steps #1, #2 and #3 is important, but now it gets even more serious when we deal with physical and mental health, merging finances from two individuals in a relationship, and integrity. In my practice, health and finances are the most difficult to deal with when people have made commitments to each other without having these areas settled prior to engagement and marriage. That's why they're last in the book. If you've made it this far, it's time to take on the tough subjects and share information with each other so you can make a good decision on whether or not to take the next step toward engagement and marriage. Having absolute integrity between two people is imperative, and a disaster when it's absent.

Marriage is an incredibly complex arrangement between two people. Bad health, whether it's physical or mental, can change an ideal relationship into what some might call a nightmare.

The number one cause for divorce is finances. It is complex and can turn negative when one or both members in a relationship are dishonest, mentally ill or incompetent money managers. When these negatives are present, the whole house of cards in a marriage can crumble into dust.

In this step we want to look at what you can do in a preparatory manner to analyze the potential for problems. As has often been said, "It's easy to fall in love. It's easy to get married. But it's not so easy to have a relationship of trust and commitment with the right person that lasts the test of time." My hope is that this final step will make a difference, so if you decide to get engaged, your chance of success and happiness will be almost guaranteed.

# STEP #4
## PHYSICAL & MENTAL HEALTH, FINANCES & INTEGRITY

1. **Preparation:**
   a. Separately read and fill out all the questionnaires in Step #4 including the page on what you would do with $25,000 with no restrictions.
   b. Fill out the budget, asset/liabilities form. Get copies of your last 2 years of Federal and State (if applicable) tax returns.

2. **Plan:**
   a. Schedule a full day that you and your partner can spend together.
   b. Find a place close by that you can take a two to three hour hike.
   c. Arrange and get permission to have a visit to your workplace and/or school for you and your partner.

3. **Activity 1: Go on a hike in the morning for 2-3 hours.**
   a. Dress appropriately and expect to expend some serious energy.
   b. Go at a pace that allows conversation. Bring along some snacks and take breaks regularly.
   c. Discuss and compare your answers to the question about the $25,000 free gift.
   d. Discuss your answers to the questionnaire on physical and mental health.

4. **Activity 2: Have lunch together. Discuss your financial condition/information.**
   a. Assuming you agree to share your financial information, sign the non-disclosure form in each of your books.
   b. Discuss and compare your budgets, assets/liabilities and your tax returns.
   c. Compare your answers to the questions about finance.

5. **Activity 3: Visit each other's workplace and/or school.** (maybe a lunch during the week)
   a. Give your partner detail on what you do for work or for school.
   b. Share with each other your career plans and hopes for the future.
   c. Discuss your answers to the questionnaire about integrity.
   d. Optionally have dinner together and discuss the events of the day.

6. **AFTER:**
   a. Record in your journal your feelings about the issues discussed in this step. How do you feel about your partner's mental and physical health? Are you in agreement with how finances should be handled? Do you feel your partner has high integrity? Are there any red flags or warning signs that need to be resolved?

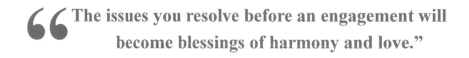

**The issues you resolve before an engagement will become blessings of harmony and love."**

# STEP #4– QUESTIONNAIRE #1
## PHYSICAL & MENTAL HEALTH ISSUES?

1. Did your parents treat you well when you were sick?

2. Did your parents believe in going to the doctor or did they prefer only home treatment? Were they strict in their medical approaches?

3. How do you feel about you or your partner taking over-the-counter drugs such as antihistamines? Sleeping pills? Cough medicine?

4. How do you feel about taking vitamins and other supplements or naturopathic or homeopathic remedies for illness?

5. Do you or your partner think that most illness is psychological? If so, why?

6. How do you want to be treated or cared for by your partner when you are ill? How about for a cold, the flu, or other illnesses? How about during pregnancy?

7. Do you feel that health insurance is important? Do you have insurance now? How do you want to handle this when you are married?

8. Do you have any chronic illnesses which you need to tell your partner? If so, what kind of help would you need from your partner?

STEP #4– QUESTIONNAIRE #1 - Continued

9.  Do you agree with your partner about medical issues or are you in conflict with each other?

10. What is your food regimen? Are you a vegan or a vegetarian? Are you the same as your partner in your eating habits or different?

11. Does your partner criticize or joke about the kinds of food you eat?

12. Do you like bland food, spicy food, organic fruits/vegetables etc.?

13. Do you have food allergies? List any.

14. Do you like many different kinds of food or a set group?

15. Do you have weight issues that you have not resolved?

16. Does your partner hound you about your weight?

17. Do you wish that your partner was thinner?

18. Are you dieting now? Do you commonly diet?

19. Have you ever suffered or currently suffer from an eating disorder? Bulimia? Anorexia? Are you trying to resolve this issue? Describe.

20. List your health history with the most important elements: e.g., childhood diseases, bone fractures, operations, etc.

21. List any hereditary illnesses that are prevalent in your family such as: ADHD, Dyslexia, Down Syndrome, Autism, Cancer, Heart Disease, Diabetes, Alzheimer's, etc.

22. If you're female, do you suffer with PMS or other menstruation related problems?

23. If your partner is female, suffering from female health issues, do you know much about the subject and how would you deal with it in a relationship?

24. Do you have a history of mental illness in your family? What kinds? Who has them?

25. Have you been treated for depression? Do you suffer from Depression now? What is the diagnosis?

26. Do you suffer from anxiety? Are you being treated for it? Describe how it affects you.

27. Have you had any other mental issues? Any personality disorders? Please list if you have one or more and how you would handle this in a relationship?

28. Have you ever cut on yourself? If so, at what age, and how often?

29. Do you currently have any sexual diseases? What are they?

30. Have you had any sexual diseases in the past? What was your treatment? What is the current prognosis?

31. Do you have any inherited illnesses? List them.

32. Have you been ill in the relationship? How did your partner treat you?

33. How many hours of sleep a night do you need?

34. Are you a morning person or a night person? Do you know this about your partner? How would you deal with conflict, if it occurs?

35. If having children and pregnancy is a possibility, what is your viewpoint on natural childbirth and Lamaze?

36. Do you expect your partner or yourself to stay home with a child through child rearing years, or return to work in a reasonable amount of time after childbirth? What is a reasonable amount of time to you?

37. Do you believe in nursing a baby or using formula? For how long?

38. If you weren't able to have children, would you consider adoption?

39. How to you feel about fertility treatments, artificial insemination?

40. How do you feel about abortion?

41. Is it important to you that your partner bathes every day?

42. Have you noticed hygiene issues with your partner? What are they?

43. Do you brush your teeth and floss twice a day? Is it important to you to have six-month dental cleanings?

44. Is it important to you that your partner uses mouthwash or other breath fresheners?

45. Is it important to you to have nails done professionally? How often?

46. How much money do you spend on haircuts, hair coloring each month?

47. How often do you have professional massages? Is this mandatory in your life?

48. Is it part of your clean health regimen to have professionally laundered shirts, blouses, skirts, dresses?

49. How important is it to you to keep up your body by participating in regular sports, attending a health club on a daily basis, or exercising on equipment at home?

50. How important is it to you to have your partner stay trim and fit?

51. How important to you is it to work out daily?

52. Do you have a gym membership you expect to keep up when you are married?

STEP #4 – QUESTIONNAIRE #1 – Continued

53. Do you believe in coloring your hair or going gray?

54. Do you believe in cosmetics or are you "au natural?"

55. How do you feel about aging and cosmetic surgery?

56. Regarding health, do you see yourself as a high maintenance or low maintenance person? Do you foresee conflicts in your relationship?

57. Do you drink alcohol? How much? How often?

58. Are you or have you ever been an alcoholic?

59. Have you had treatment for alcohol addiction? How long? How long ago? What is your status now?

60. Have you ever taken recreational drugs? What kind? How much and when?

61. Have you ever been in rehab for drug abuse?

62. If you had an addiction, are you clean from drugs/alcohol now? For how long? If not, what are you currently doing for it?

63. Are you addicted to cigarettes or nicotine vaping? If so, how much a day?

64. If you smoke or vape, do you want to quit? Does your partner object to your smoking?

65. Do you have any other substance abuse problems? If so, what?

66. Do you believe that marijuana is harmless? What do you think about studies that say it causes violent behavior?

67. Are you addicted to pornography? Do you think it should be a part of a good relationship?

68. Do you attend strip bars? Have you told your partner?

69. Do you think it's OK to go to bars alone and drink without your partner?

70. Do you think it's OK to spend time at bars with friends without your partner?

# STEP #4 – HEALTH

## DEALING WITH ADDICTION

Addiction in a relationship can be devastating. It is common for individuals to want to hide this kind of behavior fearing the relationship will end. If your partner has this problem, it's critical that it be confronted. Following is a suggested format to deal with addiction in a relationship.

### FORMAT FOR DISCUSSION
### ON ADDICTIONS

*Nelson was a college football star. At one time he injured his back and was prescribed pain medication. The modern miracle of medicine was a blessing. However, rather than getting help with tools such as meditation, yoga, Pilates, back rehabilitation therapy, and a slow weaning off of the drugs, over time he became addicted to pain medication known as opioids. The years ticked by and soon he was buying opioid drugs off the black market. He was an outstanding young man and Louisa was madly in love with him. Louisa knew about his addiction and was very concerned. It was a deal breaker to her to get engaged to someone addicted to drugs. They discussed the situation using this format to find their solution:*

## REWARD HONESTY and WILLINGNESS TO CHANGE

Louisa, "Thanks for being willing to discuss this very difficult topic. "

Nelson: "Sure. It's obvious that I need help."

Louisa: "First of all thanks for telling me the truth. Was it hard for you to admit to me that you were an addict?"

Nelson: "Yes, I was afraid if I told you that you would dump me right away. I thought about never telling you. I thought that I could keep it a secret. I've been able to hide it for so long."

## ASSURE THE ADDICT THAT YOU ARE THERE FOR THEM AS LONG AS THEY ARE TRYING TO CHANGE

Louisa: "I can understand you not wanting to tell me. Are you still concerned that I might break off our relationship now?"

Nelson: "Yes, and I can't say that I blame you."

Louisa: "I don't want to break it off. I love you so much. But I don't want to be engaged to an opioid addict either. So, what can we do to compromise?"

Nelson: "This is a situation in which there is no real compromise. I can't negotiate with you to take one pill a day and have it be ok. That would just escalate my addiction again. So I guess if I want to get engaged to you, I have to give up pain-killers.

## MAKE SURE THEY ARE WILLING TO CHANGE

Louisa: "Are you willing to take that step?"

Nelson: "I want to. I don't know if I can find a free outpatient place. I have to keep working at my job."

## OFFER CONCRETE HELP

Louisa: "Let get on the internet now……..here, are some places………shall I call these?

Nelson: "Yes, please."

Louisa spends the next 30 minutes calling around and finds the perfect place for Nelson.

## GET A COMMITMENT

Louisa: "Are you willing to commit to the next 30 days in daily outpatient treatment."

Nelson: "Yes. I am."

*In this case, Nelson wanted to overcome his addiction and was willing to do so with the help of Louisa. If there is not an agreement to change and a commitment to get professional help, you are guaranteeing heartache. If you allow your relationship to continue, you become part of the problem – evolving into co-dependency and doing great harm to both of you. (Note: Co-dependency is a behavioral condition in a relationship where one person enables another person's addiction, poor mental health, immaturity, irresponsibility, or under-achievement. Among the core characteristics of co-dependency is an excessive reliance on another person for approval and a sense of identity.)*

**The format for working with someone that has an addiction contains these elements:**

1. Discuss the addiction with the addict, rewarding honesty and a willingness to change.

2. Assure the addict that you are there for them as long as they are trying to change.

3. Make absolute sure they are willing to change.

4. Offer and deliver concrete help.

5. Get a commitment from the addict to follow the plan and offer to make sure it happens.

# STEP #4 - HEALTH
## CONCEPTS TO CONSIDER

Without good physical health habits and the support of your mate to maintain good health, it is hard to have a healthy and loving relationship. Carefully resolve your differences prior to an engagement. Seek professional and/or medical help for any unresolved health issues such as: drug addiction, sexual diseases, other addictions, and illnesses prior to your engagement. Delay commitments until you resolve these issues.

*Cassie's mother was a nurse. She had grown up with a mother who nursed her back to health when she was ill. Many times, her mother forced her to stay home from school to get well. Cassie was ambitious, thrived on schoolwork, and excelled in extracurricular activities after school. Cassie wouldn't stay home unless she was practically on her deathbed. When she married Andrew, she had no idea that he thought most illnesses were psychological. He was by nature a healthy person and had no understanding when she became ill. He would tell her that it was all in her head. As the years went by, this was a great source of contention between them. One day Cassie went to the hospital for an emergency. She was doubled over in pain. The doctors on call identified her pain as a ruptured appendix. They operated immediately to save her life. Her dogmatic husband refused to believe that the operation was necessary and refused to talk about it. They didn't have any children, so Cassie filed for divorce. Any love that she once had for Andrew had been eroded away by his intolerance.*

It is critical that you and your partner have the same philosophy on health issues.

If you are worried that your partner has an eating disorder, make sure that he/she sees a doctor and gets resolution. Delay any movement toward engagement until he/she is ready. It's worth the wait.

Are your eating habits compatible? If not, make sure that deal with the differences. You don't want to be sneaking out at night to eat a steak because your spouse is a vegetarian and disapproves.

*Charlotte wished that she had married a different man when it came to eating. Her husband was always on a new fad diet. She found herself cooking two meals each dinner. Then when the kids came along and began grade school, they noticed that their father ate differently than the rest of them. Soon, Charlotte was fixing four different meals for four fussy eaters. After fifteen years of marriage she reached her limit. She told her family that she was no longer going to fix four different meals at dinner and went on strike. Her husband started to cook for the family and after two weeks he laid down the law that everybody had to eat whatever his wife fixed, one meal only! He finally understood her plight. Fortunately, all ended happily ever after. However, this situation could have been thought out, discussed, and settled prior to marriage, avoiding fifteen years of food hell.*

If your partner is addicted to pornography it may mean that he/she will want to engage in sexual behavior that horrifies you. If he/she is addicted to drugs or alcohol, nothing good will come until the addiction is controlled and eliminated.

REMEMBER: If you cannot resolve these health-related issues prior to an engagement, it is okay to end the relationship. It may be painful for a while, but later, when you find Mister or Miss Right, you will thank yourself many times for your strength and wisdom.

# FINANCES
## STEP # 4 – QUESTIONNAIRE #2
# !FREE GIFT!

If you were given a gift of $25,000 with no strings attached, meaning you never had to pay it back, what would you spend it on?

1. _____

2. _____

3. _____

4. _____

5. _____

# STEP #4 – QUESTIONNAIRE #3
## FINANCES

**List twelve or more financial expectations you have for a future marriage including material possessions.** (Examples: kind of car and cost; kind of home and cost: cottage, mansion; living in the city; living near the ocean; being out of debt, etc. Do you expect to buy your clothes at Target or Nordstrom, etc.?)

1. _____
2. _____
3. _____
4. _____
5. _____
6. _____
7. _____
8. _____
9. _____
10. _____
11. _____
12. _____
13. _____
14. _____
15. _____

# STEP # 4 – QUESTIONNAIRE #4
## FINANCIAL PHILOSOPHIES

1. How much income would you like to make this year? In five years? In ten years?

2. Who will primarily earn the living now and later? What are your expectations for your partner's income?

3. How should financial decisions be made, separate or together? If so, how?

4. Do you use credit cards? If so, do you have credit card debt? What is your philosophy about credit cards – pay them off each month, use them as long-term credit, or just use them only for emergencies?

5. How much debt do you feel is acceptable in a marriage?

6. Are you or your partner currently in debt? What are the debts?

`f you now have debts, should you pay them off prior to marriage?
   `v will you manage paying them off?

8. Do you use a budget individually? Do you want to establish a budget together?

9. Who will manage the family finances, checkbooks, accounting, taxes, etc.?

10. Do you think you should share a checkbook or have separate accounts?

11. Should you each have an allowance or personal slush fund money that you don't have to answer for? If so, how much?

12. If you get married, should you ask each other for agreement before you spend above a certain amount like $50, $100, or $?

13. Should decisions be made by one person or together when buying things like furniture, cars, or expensive household items? When is it OK to buy on time? When should you pay cash?

14. When is it OK to go into debt to buy something you want? What is the maximum amount of debt you can tolerate?

15. Are you the kind of person who might buy something on a whim without consulting your partner? If so, do you foresee this as a problem?

16. How much money should be planned for haircuts/salon visits, etc.?

17. What do you now spend money on to keep yourself well groomed? Waxing? Nails? Massages?

18. How much money should be spent on clothing each year?

19. What is your taste in clothing? Where do you buy your clothes? Would you buy in a secondhand store? What are you willing to do for a short term if you are struggling financially? What are you not willing to do long term?

20. Would you rather spend your annual clothing allowance on a few expensive name brand items a year, or use the same budget to buy several garments at a thrift store, discount or outlet store, etc.?

21. Would you rather shop with your partner for clothing or do it yourself?

22. Do you consider yourself primarily a spender or a saver?

23. Are there any areas in which you see your partner spending money that you'd like to see done differently? For example, does he/she spend more on a hobby, clothing, recreation, vacations or cars than you think appropriate?

24. Are there areas where you would like to see your partner spend more money?

25. Do you or your partner gamble? On a regular basis? Do either of you have debts from gambling?

26. Do either of you buy lottery tickets? What is your philosophy on such purchases?

27. If you both work and earn different amounts of income, how will you share your money? Will you want to pool the money together? Or will you want some sort of separate accounting system?

28. Do you have an emergency fund in case something unplanned happens? Would you want to continue that with your partner?

29. Would you be willing to take a finance course to help you better plan financially?

# STEP #4 – ASSIGNMENT #1

**FILL OUT THIS BUDGET FORM FOR YOU FOR ONE MONTH. If you have annual or bi-annual expenses, figure out how much they would average monthly and enter that amount.**

1. Your income minus withholding taxes, etc.:     $_____
2. Any other income you receive monthly:          $_____

**3. TOTAL NET INCOME**                            $_____

## MONTHLY FIXED EXPENSES:

| | | | | |
|---|---|---|---|---|
| Rent/mortgage | $_____ | Second Mortgage | $_____ |
| Utilities: | Electricity | $_____ | Real Estate Tax | $_____ |
| | Water/Sewer | $_____ | HOA, Assn. Dues | $_____ |
| | Gas | $_____ | Phone/Cell | $_____ |
| | Garbage | $_____ | Internet | $_____ |
| Student Debt payment | $_____ | Cable, Netflix, Hulu.. | $_____ |
| Tuition | $_____ | Savings | |
| Car payment | $_____ | Emergency | $_____ |
| Car insurance | $_____ | Retirement | $_____ |
| Medical insurance | $_____ | Investment | $_____ |
| Other Insurance | $_____ | College Fund | $_____ |
| Other dues/subscriptions | $_____ | Vacation fund | $_____ |
| Other debt | $_____ | Charity | $_____ |
| Other _____ | $_____ | Licenses | $_____ |
| Other _____ | $_____ | Alimony/Child care | $_____ |

**TOTAL**     $_____

## VARIABLE EXPENSES:

| | | | | |
|---|---|---|---|---|
| Food | Groceries | $_____ | Clothing | $_____ |
| | Dining out | $_____ | Health/Medical | |
| | Emergency | $_____ | Doctors | $_____ |
| Car gasoline & oil | $_____ | Medication | $_____ |
| Car maintenance, wash, tires | $_____ | Vitamins | $_____ |
| Household | | Other | $_____ |
| | Cosmetics/Hair | $_____ | Recreation/Sports | $_____ |
| | Cleaning/laundry | $_____ | Club membership | $_____ |
| | Books/Music | $_____ | Dates/entertainment | $_____ |
| | Technology | $_____ | Childcare | $_____ |
| | Pet costs | $_____ | Child/Baby supplies | $_____ |
| | Furniture/supplies | $_____ | | |

**TOTAL**     $_____

## FINANCIAL SUMMARY

Monthly Fixed Expenses total $_____

Monthly Variable Expenses total $_____

**TOTAL MONTHLY EXPENSES** $_____

**Total Net Income** $_____

**Minus Total expenses** $_____

**Remainder** $_____

Next, fill out the financial statement below regarding your financial assets and debt.

## ASSETS

Deposits in Banks

    Checking $_____

    Savings $_____

    CD's etc. $_____

Debts owed to you:

    Personal $_____

    Other $_____

Stocks & Bonds

    _____ $_____

    _____ $_____

Real Estate Equity

    Property 1 $_____

    Property 2 $_____

Automobile value $_____

Furniture & Fixtures value $_____

Other Assets (personal)value $_____

**TOTAL ASSETS** $_____

## LIABILITIE/DEBT

Short Term Debts

    Credit card 1 $_____

    Credit card 2 $_____

    Credit card 3 $_____

Other short term debt $_____

    (taxes, etc.) $_____

Debt to relatives $_____

Other contracts $_____

     $_____

Notes payable $_____

Long Term Debts

    Real Estate $_____

    Student $_____

Other $_____

     $_____

**TOTAL DEBT** $_____

# STEP # 4 - FINANCES
## CONCEPTS TO CONSIDER

After looking at your budget, review the results in detail. Are you in the hole? If you are, then go back and cut out some of the variable expenses. When you compare your budget and financial condition with your partner, your eyes will be opened in this critical area of any relationship.

*When I was a little girl I remember vividly hearing my parents talk about the Gilmores. They were a handsome couple with a little girl named Patty, just my age. They lived in a beautiful home. I always thought it was the greatest luck in the world to play at her house. It seemed that she always had every new toy advertised on TV including: a stove that warmed up toast, a Chatty Cathy doll that talked, a small ironing board and child size iron that plugged into the wall, and a herd of plastic horses. At school I traded shoes with her. I had only one pair of brown shoes for school and church. Patty had two pairs of school shoes: one red and one brown, and a black patent leather pair for church and dress up occasions. She was rich to me. I heard my parents whisper about how the Gilmores lived beyond their means and it would catch up with them one day. I had no idea what that meant at the time.*

*Suddenly one day Patty had to move away. I heard my parents whisper that they had gone bankrupt and were getting out of town before their creditors came after them. Patty cried the day she left school. She told me that she was tired of moving every two years to a new town and school. Next thing I knew Patty and her mother were back in town without the father. The mother had changed their last name and they were now living in a tiny basement apartment in a poor section of town. After years of being married to a man who spent their family into oblivion, Mrs. Gilmore divorced, hoping to regain financial security. Fortunately, she was able to recover eventually, but never to the level that she was used to in her marriage. I don't know what happened to her husband.*

REMEMBER: Financial problems are the number one reason for divorce! It's important to feel secure in this area before you commit to a life with your partner.

*Even if you're not having problems, everyone can benefit from experts like Dave Ramsey. His financial advice in his books and programs is wonderful and will help anyone better their life.*

# STEP #4 – QUESTIONNAIRE #5
## QUESTIONS ON INTEGRITY

1. Do you have any past criminal activity that you have not already confessed to your partner? Are you hiding any other secret that would be devastating to your partner? If the answer is yes, why haven't you told him/her? What has prevented you from telling the truth?

2. Has your partner told you a lie and you later found out the truth? Was his/her explanation acceptable? Was this a one-time event, or part of a bigger problem?

3. What policies would you like to form in your relationship about telling each other the truth?  List your ideas.

4. Does your partner tell white lies? For example, if you are invited to a party that your partner doesn't want to attend, would he ask you to lie and tell them that he's sick or some other false excuse? How about the reverse?

5. Do you have a partner who has a tendency to exaggerate to you and others? Does that bother you? How have you dealt with it?

6. If a cashier gives you a ten-dollar bill by mistake rather than the actual five dollars in change owed you, would you keep it and say nothing, or feel obligated to give it back?

# STEP #4 – PHYSICAL & MENTAL HEALTH, FINANCES & INTEGRITY

## CONCEPTS TO CONSIDER

Marriage is like a business in the form of a partnership. Just like in a business, the mental and physical health of the partners is critical to success. And like a business, financial solvency and profit are essential. And of course, high integrity between the partners is mandatory. So, as you consider each other for a more permanent relationship, remember that keeping the partnership healthy is the key to happiness. You will always still remain individuals, separate in some ways – physically, mentally, spiritually, but now there is another entity – your marriage - that needs as much care as the health of the individuals involved. Unity of thought and purpose based on a clear understanding of each other's strengths and weaknesses must drive any marriage. If that falls apart, no marriage or business can survive.

Love often clouds reason. Having love for each other is important, but it cannot survive alone. Financial disasters can ruin any relationship, no matter how much two people love each other. Serious mental health issues can destroy love because they consume individuals and prevent any meaningful relationship. Dishonesty is like a cancer in marriage and will destroy the union.

Once a couple decides they are right for each other, then a thorough exploration of health, financial and integrity issues is necessary. I have seen many sincere couples that want to make their marriage work, but because of poor financial planning and lack of skills to make a living, they falter and eventually cannot carry on together. The same is true for mental health. If one partner has serious issues like bi-polar disorder or schizophrenia, they will probably need medication for their entire lives. The other partner will have to learn how to tolerate and help them – and this can become a full-time job, something rarely thought of during courtship.

I saved this step for last because it is the most critical and contains most of the serious causes of divorce and misery in marriage. Take the study of these issues and obstacles very seriously in your relationship. Complete honesty is critical. With two open, capable individuals, willing to serve and help each other, many of these obstacles can be overcome, but only if you go in with your eyes wide open.

Real life has very little to do with fairy tales. The concept that "everything will work out OK" is not true. Every relationship will have its challenges, but you must make sure that those challenges are something you can handle. If they are beyond your capability, misery results. It's best to determine if you can deal with these issues prior to marriage. So much pain in this world could be prevented if people would only take the time to make sure they know what they're getting into when they find a partner and decide to spend their life with them. May you take the time and be honest with yourself.

# CONCLUSION

**N**ow that you have completed this course, ask yourself how you can know for sure if you should get engaged and prepare for marriage. From my experience, there are two critical elements in making a successful important decision. They are: 1. The facts that you've learned about yourself and your partner and 2. The feelings you have that tell you if making a commitment

*Congratulations!*

is right or not. The second is fortified by the thorough study you make of each other. To make that final decision, I recommend that you first study out all the activity results. If you have all successes, it's a resounding "yes" to get engaged. If you have half successes and half failures, list your pros and cons of taking the next step. Make your decision in your mind only. Wait several days. Listen to your automatic internal psychological problem-solving mechanism. If you feel peaceful and good about your decision, it is your inner self telling you it's right. If on the other hand you feel confused, depressed, or generally unhappy, then it's probably not right and your inner self is telling you, "Don't get engaged." Listen to your heart and mind and see if they're saying the same thing. Both your intellectual and spiritual/emotional sides should be in agreement if it's right. Now, if you feel it's right, then your next task is to ask if your partner feels the same. If it doesn't work out, have no fear. You still have hope and certainly more knowledge on the kind of person that will be right for you.

Think about what you have learned about each other. Do you have what it takes to make a relationship that can last the test of time? The 4 steps represent building blocks with a firm foundation if you've made it through. If not, maybe you can work on a few areas and overcome your weaknesses. Or, if you discovered some problems to your unity, then you should slow down until you have the confidence to make a commitment. And if you discovered too many issues, perhaps it's time to look for someone more compatible. If so, don't look at it as a failure. It's probably just what you needed to find the right person with which to spend the rest of your life.

In my many years as a therapist, I have seen many successes and many failures. I've seen marriages rescued and I've seen them fail. It all comes down to making the principles in this book work for you every day, and when a problem arises, as it surely will, you'll hopefully have the tools and energy and love between you to find a solution. My desire is that you succeed in this most rewarding and important part of life.

If you end your relationship today, make sure that you part friends. This is not about being inferior or unworthy people. It is about being different. YOU ARE PERFECT FOR SOMEONE AND THAT SOMEONE MAY BE SOMEONE ELSE! Honor each other's differences and rejoice in the friendship you've had. Remain friends and rejoice and share in each other's joy when you each find the "one."

If you have finished this course and know that you are getting engaged or marrying the right person, all my best wishes as you begin your life together. And remember, just because you marry the right person, it doesn't mean that you won't have problems. You will, guaranteed, but at least now you are going into this engagement and future wedding with your eyes wide open and with the tools to deal with whatever comes along.

Now become a great example so you can help your friends and family when they face this same issue in their future.

APPENDIX

## APPENDIX A
# RED FLAGS

## Beware of these RED FLAGS before you make any commitments to an engagement for marriage.

1. Your partner is verbally or physically abusive and controlling.

2. You are unable to resolve conflicts and disagreements with your partner.

3. Your partner uses criticism, defensiveness, sarcasm, or refuses to talk about issues that concern you.

4. Your partner is unforgiving of little mistakes and unintentional hurts, refuses to give you compassion, understanding and instead punishes you verbally.

5. Your partner refuses to talk to you and ignores you for several days when he/she is upset at something you have done.

6. Your partner refuses to give you the kind of love that you need by not recognizing and acknowledging your love language.

7. You feel that you have to walk on eggshells to keep your partner happy.

8. You partner is emotionally mercurial, denies any mental illness problems, and is in denial about his/her issues or weaknesses.

9. Your partner has not resolved past relationships.

10. Your partner is financially irresponsible and deeply in debt.

11. Your partner is not revealing his/her past. He/she is vague, evasive, secretive, and/or insists that it's unimportant.

12. Your partner is not open and transparent about his/her daily schedule. He/she has portions of his days unaccounted for.

13. Your partner has proven to be dishonest with you and lies to others frequently.

14. You are afraid to talk about your feelings for fear of losing him/her.

15. You have not addressed, or you have ignored the objections of your friends and family.

16. You have different philosophies of life and/or religious differences that are unresolved.

17. Your partner has nothing in common with you except physical attraction.

18. Your partner loves his/her pet animal(s) more than you. He/she refuses to compromise about the pets, regardless of your allergy and health issues or your personal philosophy on pets.

19. Your partner is lazy when it comes to chores and work around the house.

20. Your partner doesn't have a job and gives excuses for not getting one.

21. Your partner displays controlling jealousy and has you on a short leash.

# APPENDIX B
# BONUS SECTION

❧⌘❧

# GOAL PLANNING

❝ **Successful couples have annual goal planning sessions to write out their goals.** ❞

**Now assuming that you've found the right person, get together and list your goals as you would like to have them for your first year of marriage in the following categories:**

1. Financial/Career

2. Spiritual

3. Intellectual/Educational

4. Social

5. Family

6. Physical

## List five-year and ten-year goals in the same areas:

Financial/Career

Spiritual

Intellectual/Educational

Social

Family

Physical

# BONUS ACTIVITY – GOAL SETTING
## CONCEPTS TO CONSIDER

How did your goal planning session go? Are you able to work together easily? Did your partner take the goal planning session seriously? Do you have the same goals? Are you eager to support each other's goals? Do you feel that you have a mission together? Do you feel that you have a destiny together? Are you excited about the things that you have planned together? Are you committed to making each other's dreams and goals come true? These are important issues that will affect your relationship for years to come.

*Stephanie had dreamed of being an author her whole life. She made up stories to entertain children. She wrote novelettes in high school and college. She wrote in her journal at age sixteen, "I will become a published author by age thirty. I will earn a living writing books by age forty."*

*Stephanie married right out of college. She never talked about her goals with her husband. When the children came, she spent hours writing at home. Her husband had little tolerance for the time she spent writing. He was the antithesis of supportive. He berated her, nagged her, and tried to sabotage her efforts. Finally, she divorced him. Now saddled with the primary care of her two children and a new financial burden, she taught school by day and wrote by night. At age thirty-two she published her first novel for teenagers. By forty she was a popular author adored by teenage girls earning a half a million dollars a year! When her husband found out, he came after her with a saber-toothed lawyer, hungry to claim part of her earnings. What was his claim? "I supported her for years while she was writing at home." His case was thrown out.*

How sad it was that her husband couldn't buy into her goals and support her emotionally when they were married. The moral of the story is: marry someone who enjoys setting goals, who will support your goals, buy into your mission on earth, and rejoice in the success you achieve in the goals you set individually and together.

**MAKE A COMMITMENT TO HAVE AN ANNUAL GOAL PLANNING SESSION AND YOU WILL ACCOMPLISH GREAT THINGS TOGETHER!**

# BONUS ACTIVITY
# ANIMALS AND PETS

This is an important issue if it applies to your relationship. If one or both of you have a pet or pets, it's important to talk with your partner about the importance of pets in your life. If it's a dog, maybe go to a dog park together and discuss how the dog will play a part in your relationship. This may seem insignificant, but I guarantee you, it is not. Fill out this questionnaire and discuss.

1. Do you like animals?

2. Do you have a pet currently? What is it?

3. Do you intend on having a dog or cat when you are in a relationship and married? Or other animals? If so what? How many?

4. Do you sleep with a pet on your bed at night?

5. Are you allergic to pets? Are you allergic to dog hair or cat fur? If so, what does your partner expect you to do if he/she owns a dog/cat? Is this a deal breaker in the relationship?

6. What are your philosophies on pets living in the home? Outside the home?

7. If you partner has a pet that lives in the house and you don't like that, how will you compromise?

# BONUS ACTIVITY
# FOR SENIORS ONLY

**Following are some issues for Seniors that need to be revealed and discussed before two older people get engaged and married.**

## FINANCES:

Finances can be complex between two Seniors. Acknowledge that you need to decide an approach for the following:

1. Consider a prenuptial agreement ("prenup") which is a written contract created before two people are married. It typically lists all of the property each person owns (as well as any debts) and specifies what each person's rights will be after the marriage.
2. Discuss whether you will keep finances separated or combined once you are married.
3. Discuss if what you both earn after the marriage is shared.
4. Consider separate trusts so your assets go to whom you want when you pass.

If your partner refuses to reveal his/her finances to you, DO NOT GET ENGAGED. A senior couple who came to me for couples counseling wanted a divorce. The woman refused to reveal her finances prior to the marriage. The man was so intoxicated with her beauty he let it slide. After the marriage he found out that she had gone bankrupt once and now had a debt of $90,000. Due to the laws of their state, he was now responsible for her debt.

## INTIMACY:

1. Are you both in working order?
2. Has the woman been through some other physical issues and has no interest in sex? Or is she willing to find some natural or medical means to resolve the physical issues for her partner? Make sure you discuss.
3. Is the man impotent, but able to do something medicinally to correct that?
4. Whatever is occurring in this area, it's important to have a frank and open discussion.

## PAST RELATIONSHIPS

1. Address any issues from previous marriages that were intolerable.
2. Do you expect your new relationship to be the love of your life?
3. Do you expect your new partner to pick up where your deceased spouse left off?
4. If your partner had children, what will be their relationship, legal authority, inheritance, etc.? And what about yours?

## AGE DIFFERENCES

1. Realize that if you have a wide age difference (15 years or more) that you might not understand what your partner is talking about sometimes because of generation differences.
2. You may find out that your levels of energy are quite different.
3. If you are younger, it may happen that you will have to be a nursemaid to your partner in the future. This could last for many years.

# FOR SENIORS ONLY
# CONCEPTS TO CONSIDER

*Paul was a 70 year-old man with some minor health issues. His wife passed away due to a prolonged illness during which she was "out of commission" sexually for several years. Paul was sad that his wife of 45 years was gone but longed to remarry and resume a partnership with sexual intimacy. He had his eye on several single women in his Christian church congregation. One, I'll call Maria, stood out and he was thunderstruck with love. Paul knew that Maria's house cleaning business was not doing well and he was happy to be her sole support. Paul owned a successful constuction company and had no financial worries. He lived in a large upper middle-class home, so Maria assumed life would be perfect with Paul. Paul sent her flowers often, courted her in expensive restaurants, and proposed after one month.  They eloped after only knowing each other for two months. First, Maria was upset that Paul wouldn't let her rearrange the home and make it her own. She had to obtain a storage unit to house her furniture. She thought, "Well, I will give the furniture to my children when they get settled." Next Paul started getting upset that she didn't seem to know how to cook. He was used to a homemaker who cooked breakfast, lunch and dinner for him with organic foods. Maria was equally upset with Paul. She didn't realize that having his business in their home would make her feel as if she had no privacy. Paul's construction supervisors and his children, who worked for him, had keys to the house and would enter and exit all throughout the day. Why did she not know that? Paul was set in his ways and didn't want to create a safe place in the home for Maria during the day.*

*Maria didn't understand Paul's jokes She was from Spain. Maria wanted to go dancing with Paul, but Paul was struggling with arthritis and failed to disclose it to Maria prior to the marriage. Need I say more? This couple did not do their homework. But because they had a Christian covenant marriage, they resigned themselves to a life of quiet desperation and a life of unhappiness with each other.*

Just because you've been married before does not make you an expert. As a Senior, the process to determine if you should get engaged and married is the same as when you were first married, and perhaps even more complicated because of habits and customs that are cast in stone and probably impossible to change.

# IMPROMPTU VISIT

*(If you are having doubts about honesty and integrity, this might be a good idea.)*

**BEFORE:** Plan a time when you know your partner will be home. Do not tell him/her you are coming to visit.

**INSTRUCTIONS:** Show up unexpectedly.

**AFTER:** Fill out the following questionnaire.

1. Was your partner angry at you for dropping in unannounced? Why?

2. Was your partner with another woman/man?

3. Was your partner's place a mess? Could this be a problem for your style of living?

4. Did he/she have something to hide that you observed?

YOUR JOURNAL

_____

DATE

Journal Date _____

## STEP #1

Notes: _____
_____
_____
_____
_____
_____

Summary: _____
_____
_____
_____
_____

What did you learn new on this activity? _____
_____
_____
_____
_____
_____

Do you have any unresolved issues in this area? What are they?
_____
_____
_____
_____

What plans do you have for resolution of these issues?
_____
_____
_____
_____

JOURNAL DATE _____

## STEP #2

NOTES: _____

_____

_____

_____

_____

_____

_____

SUMMARY: _____

_____

_____

_____

_____

WHAT DID YOU LEARN NEW ON THIS ACTIVITY? _____

_____

_____

_____

_____

_____

DO YOU HAVE ANY UNRESOLVED ISSUES IN THIS AREA? WHAT ARE THEY?

_____

_____

_____

_____

WHAT PLANS DO YOU HAVE FOR RESOLUTION OF THESE ISSUES?

_____

_____

_____

_____

JOURNAL DATE _____

## STEP #3

NOTES: _____
_____
_____
_____
_____
_____

SUMMARY: _____
_____
_____
_____
_____

WHAT DID YOU LEARN NEW ON THIS ACTIVITY? _____
_____
_____
_____
_____
_____

DO YOU HAVE ANY UNRESOLVED ISSUES IN THIS AREA? WHAT ARE THEY?
_____
_____
_____
_____

WHAT PLANS DO YOU HAVE FOR RESOLUTION OF THESE ISSUES?
_____
_____
_____
_____

JOURNAL DATE _____

STEP #4

NOTES: _____

_____

_____

_____

_____

_____

SUMMARY: _____

_____

_____

_____

_____

WHAT DID YOU LEARN NEW ON THIS ACTIVITY? _____

_____

_____

_____

_____

DO YOU HAVE ANY UNRESOLVED ISSUES IN THIS AREA? WHAT ARE THEY?

_____

_____

_____

_____

WHAT PLANS DO YOU HAVE FOR RESOLUTION OF THESE ISSUES?

_____

_____

_____

_____

# Certificate of Completion

## *The Four Step Relationship Course*

Has successfully completed the four step engagement preparation course and is certified able to make great decisions regarding relationships

This _____ Day

of _____ _____

www.LauraDenke.com